BRITISH POLICY AND THE REFUGEES 1933–1941

'When I contemplate the natural dignity of man; when I feel (for Nature has not been kind enough to me to blunt my feelings) for the honour and happiness of its character, I become irritated at the attempt to govern mankind by force and fraud, as if they were all knaves and fools, and can scarcely avoid disgust at those who are thus imposed upon.'

Thomas Paine (*Rights of Man*)

BRITISH POLICY AND THE REFUGEES
1933–1941

YVONNE KAPP and
MARGARET MYNATT

With a Foreword by Charmian Brinson

FRANK CASS
LONDON • PORTLAND, OR

First Published in 1997 in Great Britain by
FRANK CASS & CO. LTD.
Newbury House, 900 Eastern Avenue
London IG2 7HH

and in the United States of America by
FRANK CASS
c/o ISBS, 5804 N.E. Hassalo Street
Portland, Oregon 97213-3644

British Library Cataloguing in Publication Data:

Kapp, Yvonne
British policy and the refugees, 1933–1941
1. Refugees – Government policy – Great Britain – History – 20th century
I. Title II. Mynatt, Margaret
325.2'1'0941'09043

ISBN 0-7146-4797-7 (cloth)
ISBN 0-7146-4352-1 (paper)

Library of Congress Cataloging-in-Publication Data:

A catalog record for this book is available
from the Library of Congress

Typeset by
Vitaset, Paddock Wood, Kent
Printed in Great Britain by
Bookcraft (Bath) Ltd, Midsomer Norton, Avon

Contents

Part Two
THE REFUGEE PROBLEM IN WARTIME

Dedicated to the Memory of
Margaret (Bianca) Mynatt, 1907–1977

1996 Foreword

British Policy and the Refugees, largely written during the second half of 1940, came about at the time of Britain's lowest ebb in the fight against National Socialist Germany. April, May and June 1940 had witnessed dramatic and ominous events on the continent: one by one, Denmark, Norway, Holland, Belgium and France had been invaded by the German Army and, falling in quick succession, now formed part of German-occupied Europe. In late May and early June the British Expeditionary Force had had to be evacuated from Dunkirk with considerable loss of life as well as very serious losses in equipment. To many it seemed merely a matter of time until Britain, too, would be invaded.

The political events in Germany in the preceding seven years, the period of Nazi supremacy there, had resulted in large numbers of Jewish and political refugees from Germany, Austria and Czechoslovakia seeking refuge in those European countries that had since fallen to Germany or, as in Britain, were anxiously facing such a prospect. In France, in fact, almost all adult male German residents had been arrested at the outbreak of war, regardless of the status of the majority of them as refugees from Nazi oppression. In his influential *Germany: Jekyll and Hyde*, Sebastian Haffner, in exile in Britain, had condemned France's attitude to its potential allies in the fight against Nazism as a 'catastrophic defeat on the psychological battle field' and had maintained further:

> The internment of German emigrants is not a trifling bureaucratic lapse, but a deliberate political gesture. It says more clearly than any ministerial speech that the war is being waged against the German people, including those who have proved themselves anti-Hitlerian and friendly to the Allies.[1]

As the present study indicates, the containment of the upwards of 70,000 German-speaking refugees in exile in Britain proceeded initially in a rather less hasty manner. On the outbreak of war, a few hundred enemy aliens were interned as an immediate security measure while the remainder were soon afterwards categorised by tribunals according to their perceived degree of security risk (with 'A' indicating a high risk factor, 'B' that some uncertainty could be held to exist and 'C' that loyalty to the British cause was not in question). Category 'A' aliens were then also interned, category 'B' were subject to certain restrictions, while category 'C' – by far the majority – continued to enjoy unrestricted freedom. 'The principles', as the authors of this book, Yvonne Kapp and Margaret Mynatt, themselves concede, 'were reasonable.' Yet, on an individual level, there were very many instances where the system was patently unjust, attended as it was by much confusion and ignorance as well as by inconsistencies from tribunal to tribunal. For example, some tribunals took a highly unfavourable view of socialist or communist refugees who came up before them – regardless of the impeccable anti-Nazi record many of them enjoyed – and categorised them accordingly. Indeed, to cite only one such case, in March 1940 the *New Statesman and Nation* was moved to speak out against the treatment meted out at a Hampstead tribunal to the noted economist and statistician Jürgen Kuczynski, who had previously been active in the communist underground in Nazi Germany, and his father, the population expert R. R. Kuczynski, then lecturing at the London School of Economics:

> I cannot understand why R. R. Kuczynski could ever have come under suspicion at all, as he is a researcher with a world-wide reputation, and has never had any connections with a political party. But the judge seemed to find grounds for suspicion even in his trips to America and asked him, to the old man's surprise, whether he had any connection with an espionage system in Bloomsbury House! Finally, in summing up his case, the judge remarked 'I am not going to intern you *to-day*,' and in granting his wife a 'B' certificate stated that the ground was that she was living under the subversive influence of her husband. When her husband protested and reminded the judge that he was teaching at the London School of Economics, the judge replied ominously, 'I know all about the London School of Economics.' J. Kuczynski was subjected to an even severer cross-examination. It seemed to be held against him

> that he had written *Hunger and Work* and *Freedom Calling*, although the Ministry of Information has given the latter pamphlet its blessing ... He was also pestered about the mysterious espionage system in Bloomsbury House, and when he replied that he had no connection with it, the judge added 'That doesn't answer the question, you might be connected with someone who was connected with the espionage system.' The result of this remarkable examination was a 'B' licence for the elder and internment for the younger Kuczynski. The judge seemed suspicious of any trace of anti-Nazi activity ...[2]

Nevertheless, unlike in France, the majority of the refugees from Nazi oppression were left at liberty in Britain until mid-1940 when, in the face of the alarming war situation and the – almost certainly unfounded – rumours of fifth-columnist activities amongst the refugees in the occupied countries, the British military leadership and security services, together with a number of British public figures, called for the mass internment of aliens. In this, they were assisted by sections of the British press which, in April and May 1940, began to conduct an aggressive campaign against the German refugees: the *Daily Mail*, for one, which throughout the 1930s had been more than sympathetic to the rise of fascism, now maintained in its notorious Ward Price article of 24 May 1940 that it was time to despatch 'all refugees from Austria, Germany and Czechoslovakia, men and women alike ... without delay to a remote part of the country' and keep them there 'under strict supervision' since, as the 'head of a Balkan State' had allegedly opined, '*every* German is an agent'.[3] A few days later an equally notorious article appeared in the *Sunday Chronicle* in which Beverley Nichols, another leading pro-Nazi journalist of the 1930s, would demand the immediate internment of all German and Austrian refugees, on the following grounds:

> Why should we be blown up as we are walking over a bridge unless it is strictly necessary? Or poisoned by contaminated water, or hit on the head by the local gasworks, as it descends to earth? No, sir. The letters readers send about Germans who are going free in their own district would make your hair stand on end. Particularly the women. There is no dirty trick that Hitler would not do, and there is a very considerable amount of evidence to suggest that some of the women – who are very pretty – are not above offering their charms to any young man who may

> care to take them, particularly if he works in a munition factory or a public works.[4]

In fact, by May 1940 the internment of further groups of refugees was already well under way: first, male Germans and Austrians living in coastal areas were rounded up; then those who had been placed in category 'B'; next the category 'B' women. On 10 June, following Mussolini's entry into the war, over 4,000 Italians were interned, including – as in the case of the Germans and Austrians – quite a number of anti-fascist refugees among them. Finally, in the second half of June, internment was extended to category 'C' German and Austrian males, thus even to those who had been recognised indisputably as refugees from Nazi oppression and as of unquestionable loyalty to Britain.

That British officialdom should turn on such a vulnerable section of the community soon gave rise to bitter criticism, however, in those sections of the press, such as the *Manchester Guardian*, which had consistently championed the refugees, as well as in Parliament and among the British public at large. 'Why not lock up General de Gaulle?' wrote Michael Foot on 17 July in a biting article in the *Evening Standard* before putting in a plea for 'all who can give proof of their solid anti-Nazi and anti-Fascist resolution' to be 'welcomed by us as treasured allies'.[5] Eleven days later, under the title 'J'accuse', H. G. Wells also lodged a passionate protest against the official treatment of the refugees:

> This accusation I make, and make in the plainest terms. In this country, as in France before reaction threw aside all pretence, a deliberate and systematic intimidation of liberal-minded foreigners is going on. So that even while we are actually at war with the Axis Powers and their subjugated 'allies', people in positions of authority and advantage in this country are allowing the collection, internment and ill-treatment of all those disaffected subjects of our enemies who would be most willing and able to organize internal resistance in their own countries on our behalf.[6]

The subsequent British deportation policy and, in particular, the loss of life on the ill-fated *Arandora Star*, served to fuel the protests that were voiced in the House of Commons in the celebrated debate of 10 July, and elsewhere. Books on the subject appeared, chief among them *Anderson's Prisoners* by 'Judex'[7] and François Lafitte's *The Internment of Aliens*,[8] which played their part in influencing public opinion against the policy of mass internment while also pointing to the general increase in authoritarianism in Britain as revealed 'not merely in the treatment of "enemy aliens", but also in a distinct tendency to whittle away the traditional civil rights of British citizens'.[9] Yvonne Kapp and Margaret Mynatt's book, which, while addressing a broader range of refugee issues than either 'Judex' or Lafitte, was compiled at almost exactly the same time, can be read as part of this protest.

* * *

British Policy and the Refugees was written by two extraordinary women who were themselves inextricably caught up in the events of the time. As committed communists, they, like the refugees they were championing, had been badly affected by the hardening in British official policy; indeed, the period of the German–Soviet Non-Aggression Pact proved to be a testing time for all anti-fascists of communist persuasion in Britain, refugees and non-refugees alike. In their 1968 Foreword to this volume, Kapp and Mynatt relate how, in May 1940, they were dismissed from the leading positions they held in the government-sponsored Czech Refugee Trust Fund in an 'apparently isolated instance of victimisation' which 'was subsequently seen to be merely a prelude to the wholesale arrest of the refugees themselves'. Moving to Westmoreland together, they decided 'at the moment when the role and the fate of refugees in this country were a burning issue' to write the present account, to be based on their exceptional experience and involvement with refugees and refugee organisations. They did this for the most part over the next few months, merely checking and amplifying the material after their return to London at the end of 1940.

Yvonne Kapp is probably best known today for her brilliant biography of Eleanor Marx which appeared in two volumes in 1972 and 1976,[10] years after the events that are under discussion here. In a number of interviews conducted over the past few years,[11] she has described the circumstances of her childhood and youth.

She was born Yvonne Mayer in Dulwich in 1903 into a Jewish middle-class family with whom she did not always see eye to eye.

Suffering from tuberculosis, she passed a great deal of time as a child in reading and writing. Against the wishes of her parents, she went on to study journalism at King's College London and to marry a penniless artist, Edmond Kapp, working as a journalist and writer throughout the 1920s. She has also described the shift from the relatively carefree and uncommitted life she led at this period to her deeply serious and, above all, political existence in the 1930s. It was, she told Sally Alexander, the result of 'fascism in Germany and the burning of the books that as a liberal, and a Jewish liberal at that, I began to feel really involved'.[12] Then, in 1935, she visited the Soviet Union. This, followed by a meeting with the General Secretary of the British Communist Party, Harry Pollitt, led to her joining the Communist Party herself and to her years as a political activist. In 1937, for instance, she organised the now legendary Albert Hall meeting in aid of the Basque children at which Paul Robeson sang and for which Picasso donated one of his preliminary sketches for *Guernica*.

As for the refugees from Hitler, Kapp started to involve herself in relief work on their behalf from 1933 onwards, offering accommodation in her own house to a series of exiles. In 1938 she began to work full time for the hard-pressed Jewish Refugees Committee at Woburn House (later at Bloomsbury House), heading the department for refugee doctors and dentists who were seeking to come to Britain. By the time war broke out, however, she had been seconded to the British Committee for Refugees from Czechoslovakia (later known as the Czech Refugee Trust Fund), established after the invasion of Czechoslovakia with British government money for the support of Sudeten German refugees in Britain, as well as for Reich Germans and Austrians who had sought refuge in Czechoslovakia and for exiled Czechs and Slovaks (about 8,000 in total). Here, Yvonne Kapp became Assistant to the Director, the retired civil servant Sir Henry Bunbury, as well as Secretary to the Trust Fund's three trustees.

Many of the refugees under the Czech Refugee Trust Fund's aegis had formerly worked in trades or professions that were not much in demand in wartime. Yvonne Kapp 'set about devising a programme for those of active age to be drafted into industry or agriculture, including retraining for such occupations'. She was very successful. 'By the early spring of 1940', she reports, 'hundreds of the Germans, Austrians and Czechs had been drafted into factories, foundries, mines, forestry and farming.'[13] It was while she was working on her employment scheme that she was summoned to London to a meeting, called by a representative of the Home Office, ostensibly to be questioned on the *bona fides* of certain refugees employed by the Trust. It soon became clear, however, that it was primarily she who was under investigation. Sir Henry Bunbury was also interviewed about her at some length and was obliged to ask her 'whether I was or had ever been a member of the Communist Party'. Events came to a head at the Trustees' next meeting:

> I was asked to wait outside the room where we usually foregathered and spent an uncomfortable half-hour before being invited to enter when I was formally addressed by the Chairman, Sir Malcolm Delevingne. In a doleful voice he announced that with deep regret he had to inform me of the Secretary of State's decree that I should no longer work for the Trust in any capacity. They, the Trustees, who had the fullest confidence in my loyalty and integrity, would be profoundly sorry to lose my services, and he advised me to write to the Home Secretary appealing against the decision.[14]

Her appeal, however, drafted with the help of Sir Malcolm himself, failed to change the situation.

Margaret (formerly Bianca) Mynatt came from a very different background. She was born in Vienna in 1907, the daughter of an Austrian Jewish mother and a British musician (who had changed his name to Minotti for professional purposes before abandoning his family).[15] Margaret Mynatt, who grew up in the utmost poverty, had originally hoped to become a musician herself but the family had lacked the means necessary for her training. In 1929 she moved to Berlin, where she worked as a journalist – reportedly for *Die Rote Fahne, Berlin am Morgen* and *Welt am Abend* – joined the KPD (the German Communist Party) and formed part of the circle around Bertolt Brecht. Besides becoming a life-long friend of Brecht's collaborator, Elisabeth Hauptmann, Mynatt herself is said to have assisted in the creation of Brecht's *Saint Joan of the Stockyards* and other works.

After the Reichstag fire, Mynatt fled to Prague together with the graphic artist John Heartfield and others. She was briefly imprisoned there before fleeing to Paris and then, by virtue of her British passport, to London. With almost no English at her disposal, however, life was initially very hard. She managed to work intermittently as a teacher of German and as a researcher. One of her more sensitive assignments between 1936 and 1938 was to gather material for an American journalist, Clara Leiser, on the largely unexplained deaths in British exile of the German political émigrées Dora Fabian and Mathilde Wurm in 1935,[16] while she was at one stage employed by an historian to work on Dutch manuscripts in the British Museum. She also acted as a courier for the British Communist Party as well as working on a voluntary basis for anti-fascist aid organisations.

With the setting up of the British Committee for Refugees from Czechoslovakia, Yvonne Kapp relates, 'Margaret was taken on as a paid employee on the strength of her wide knowledge of refugee problems.' Initially the emphasis was on rescuing those refugees who were still stranded in Czechoslovakia, and in this connection Emmy Koenen has described Mynatt as 'the heart and soul of our entire enterprise'.[17] Later Margaret Mynatt was put in charge of the department preparing material for the tribunals where, according to Yvonne Kapp again, 'her intimate experience of refugees and political understanding of their background proved invaluable to the authorities'. In May 1940, Mynatt, like Kapp, was dismissed from her post on political grounds by order of the Home Secretary.

The two women had first met one another in 1937 in connection with Yvonne Kapp's Albert Hall meeting. However, it was through John Heartfield, and more specifically his arrival in Britain in 1938, that the life-long friendship between them was to come about. After Margaret Mynatt had left Prague some years before, she had remained in touch with Heartfield, and his brother Wieland Herzfelde's publishing firm, the celebrated Malik Verlag, was registered in London under Mynatt's name. Late in 1938, when the political refugees were being evacuated from Prague, Margaret Mynatt asked Yvonne Kapp to provide Heartfield – as 'a very special refugee' – with accommodation. The story of Heartfield's arrival is well worth the telling: he turned up exhausted one evening – Kapp had in fact been expecting him daily for the best part of a week – and, refusing all offers of food, went straight to his room. As Kapp relates it:

> The next morning at about eight o'clock I took up a breakfast tray. I knocked at the door. No answer, so I thought, 'Oh well, he's sleeping'. I went up every hour and I could not get an answer so at about eleven o'clock I rang up the people who'd originally told me this special refugee was coming and I said, 'I think your special refugee is dead. Would you come round with a strong young man who will break the door down because I can't open it.' And that's what they did. Came round and broke the door down, and there was Johnny sleeping like a baby. This was at twelve and he'd been sleeping since nine the evening before. I suppose it was the first quiet night he'd had in years.[18]

It was whilst awaiting the outcome of the forced entry into Heartfield's room that Yvonne Kapp and Margaret Mynatt really got to know one another. After the outbreak of war both women, with the rest of the Trust Fund's staff, were evacuated first to Hertfordshire, then to Berkshire, where at the time of their dismissal in May 1940 they were living in a decrepit Victorian vicarage. As Kapp recalls:

> Sir Henry posted a notice announcing our dismissal and declaring his personal regret. For a week or more, debarred from our offices, we held court in the vicarage, to which many members of the staff came with little offerings and friendly words. Then with six months' salary in lieu of notice and a glowing testimonial both from Sir Henry and also the Trustees, together with Margaret, I left for the Lake District.[19]

It perhaps remains to note here that, reluctant to be absent from London for too long, Yvonne Kapp and Margaret Mynatt returned there before the end of 1940, and that their situation, like that of their fellow Party members, underwent a complete change after the Soviet Union's entry into the war in June of the following year. Yvonne Kapp became the research officer of the Amalgamated Engineering Union and, after the war, was employed by the Medical Research Council while working as a translator in her spare time. Today she lives in Highgate. Margaret Mynatt made her career in journalism and publishing. She was in turn the founder and head of the Soviet Monitor (a round-the-clock radio service supplying news from Russia to the world press), the managing director of Central Books, a director of Lawrence & Wishart and the editor-in-chief of the English edition of the *Collected Works* of Marx and

Engels. She died of cancer in London in 1977, having for many years shared a house with her friend and co-author Yvonne Kapp.

* * *

In their temporary exile in the Lake District, the two women set about their joint project of exposing the 'present treatment of refugees in this country'. In so doing, it was Yvonne Kapp who took on most of the writing, Margaret Mynatt who was responsible for much of the factual research. The book, as the authors record in their 1968 Foreword, had already been accepted for publication when, in November 1940, a Penguin Special appeared which 'was thought to meet the demand for any book on refugees', namely the best-selling volume *The Internment of Aliens* (by the young PEP (Political and Economic Planning) researcher, committed anti-fascist and ex-communist, François Lafitte) and the proposal to publish *British Policy and the Refugees* was dropped. The paper restrictions of the time would undoubtedly have played their part here, too, while it is also possible, as Yvonne Kapp surmised in a recent interview, that their publisher had initially failed to realise the force of the attack on the British government that would be contained in *British Policy and the Refugees*.[20] Publication of this study was reconsidered in the 1960s (hence the compilation of the 1968 Foreword) and again in the 1980s but, despite the fact that, even in manuscript form, the work attracted considerable scholarly attention, a further 12 years would elapse – 57 years in total – before its eventual appearance.

Of course, Kapp and Mynatt, 'Judex' (in fact the leading Fabian and later Labour MP, Hector Delauney Hughes) and Lafitte, writing in 1940, all lacked access to the official records on the internment of aliens on which more recent studies have been able to draw. The chief sources of information open to them in 1940 were the contemporary press – although, under wartime conditions, this was largely silent on the circumstances in which internment and deportation were being carried out – reports of parliamentary proceedings and official papers and, most important, word of mouth. Lafitte has written in recent years of the information he received from refugees at the London Austrian Centre.[21] Yvonne Kapp and Margaret Mynatt, for their part, enjoyed an extensive network of contacts in the Czech Refugee Trust Fund and, even after their departure from London, succeeded in remaining exceptionally well informed on day-to-day developments within the beleaguered refugee community: thus, to take one example, it was the 'eyewitness accounts of friends among the interned refugees' that formed the basis of the Kapp/Mynatt exposition of the confusion attending the *Arandora Star*'s passenger list.

It is clearly to be expected that these three contemporary studies, while certainly of rather different political complexions, should bear some similarity to one another in their general tone and thrust. However, it is interesting to note that the conspiracy theories of internment that were rife in British left-wing circles during 1940 (which held that right-wing members of the British Establishment, as a panic measure, were endeavouring to cover up their own subversive 'fifth-column' activities by incriminating the refugees), although very much to the fore in 'Judex' and Lafitte, constitute a rather less prominent feature of the Kapp/Mynatt account; for this takes a considerably longer-term view of the refugee question in Britain. Of the studies that have appeared since selected government records on internment began to be released in 1972,[22] Peter and Leni Gillman's *'Collar the Lot!'* has played a particularly important role in examining the internal government debate on the enemy aliens. In the event, their research and that of other recent researchers does not bear out the conspiracy theories of the day; it does, however, underline the undemocratic, secretive and illiberal nature of the British treatment of the refugees, which is, of course, very much the contention of the present volume.

Yvonne Kapp and Margaret Mynatt's *British Policy and the Refugees* also makes its own quite distinct contribution, firstly to the literature of internment and deportation and, secondly, to an even more marked extent, to the study of German-speaking refugees in Britain in the years leading up to mass alien internment. On the first count, Hans Jaeger observed in 1955 that the writers who had discussed the internment problem up to that date could be divided into two categories, namely 'those who reported from outside' and 'those with "inside information"'.[23] Yvonne Kapp and Margaret Mynatt, perhaps uniquely, can be said to bridge that divide. Moreover, 30 years later, Paul Hoch would observe:

> Do not the internments have to be analyzed *both* in relation to the immediate political circumstances in which they occurred *and* also in

> relation to the longer-term underlying attitudes about foreigners and Jews which made these events possible? This has seldom, if ever, been done.[24]

It is, of course, precisely this that *British Policy and the Refugees* sets out to do.[25]

For the internments were not, to quote Paul Hoch further, 'a mere aberration performed in the heat of a particular set of circumstances', nor was 'the fact that the overwhelming majority of internees were foreign and Jewish' incidental.[26] Rather, and this is the second area and the one in which the Kapp/Mynatt study is at its most incisive, the policy of internment was fuelled by the British attitudes towards foreigners and Jews that were prevalent in Britain throughout the 1930s and before. As the anonymous 'Scipio' maintained in another influential Gollancz volume of 1940, *100,000,000 Allies – If We Choose*, 'the history of British policy towards the victims of Nazi persecution is an unedifying one'.[27] Yvonne Kapp and Margaret Mynatt's brilliant polemic – which in 1985 Nicholas Jacobs described as 'possibly the only work that attempts to deal with the political aspects of the emigration from Nazi Germany to Britain as a whole'[28] – details the 'inhumane policies' that had been the British response to the refugees from Nazi oppression since 1933: the tight restrictions on immigration, residence, employment and even on political activity in Britain, and the emphasis on future migration overseas. The picture is a bleak one:

> It has been said by experienced workers in this field that the moment of arrival in this country was the only happy one the refugees ever knew. That may be an exaggeration, but there can be no doubt that a gradual and grievous deterioration set in for many of them when, after the first overwhelming relief of being safely out of a Nazi country had worn off, they were harried and frustrated at every step.

While Kapp and Mynatt by no means plead for the unlimited and unconditional admission of aliens to Britain, they argue strongly for 'an immigration law based upon the principle of the right of asylum' – in other words, for a 'consistent pro-refugee policy' rather than the existing 'anti-refugee policy with loopholes'. At the same time, they draw a sharp distinction throughout between the inadequate official British response to the refugees and the generosity of the general public, the latter having manifested itself in remarkable fund-raising successes and in the works of the refugee relief organisations as well as in the efforts of countless little-known voluntary committees.

It is, in fact, in just this consideration of the refugee movement in Britain that *British Policy and the Refugees* is most authoritative, its authors having of course become experienced in every aspect of it in their years of work in the field. As Yvonne Kapp herself stated recently, she and Margaret Mynatt had had unique 'access to the very heart of how it was being run',[29] which, together with Margaret Mynatt's knowledge of the background, gained from bitter personal experience, made for an exceptionally illuminating account. In particular, as Tony Kushner has remarked, the book offers a critical inside perspective on an area that has been relatively neglected to date, namely the day-to-day workings of the Czech refugee organisations and of the Czech refugee movement as a whole.[30] Yvonne Kapp and Margaret Mynatt's impassioned firsthand account of the rescue of some of the refugees from Czechoslovakia – and of the fate of those who failed to reach safety – remains one of the most memorable in the book.

Kapp and Mynatt also appeal passionately on behalf of those refugees who, while unquestionably victims of Nazi oppression, had – like the above-mentioned Jürgen Kuczynski – encountered prejudice in Britain on account of their left-wing political views. At the tribunals, they relate, 'it sometimes happened that the refugee was asked if he would be prepared to take up arms against the Soviet Union ... and if he said he was not, he was automatically included in category "A" as hostile'. It is at this point, clearly, that the plight of the subject of this book comes closest to that of the authors, as Yvonne Kapp has herself intimated elsewhere:

> From the start I had taken my victimization badly. I thought it sinister and unjust, in the same way that I deplored the detention of the refugees as a disgrace.[31]

Thus the plea for the political refugees contained in this volume can be viewed as a plea, too, for other groups that had become objects of official suspicion, such as the British communists, certainly, but also the pacifists, trades unionists and other radicals.

It has already been noted that, to quote from the Kapp/Mynatt 1968 Foreword, 'with the Nazi attack on the Soviet Union in June 1941, the political situation was entirely transformed'. Interestingly, and although such a conflict is not articulated in the present volume, Yvonne Kapp has spoken of the 'appalling confusion' she experienced after the signing of the Nazi–Soviet Pact and over her belief that, contrary to what was being decreed by Party doctrine, the war was actually an anti-fascist rather than an imperialist one.[32] Of course, the fact that Harry Pollitt himself promoted the same view for a while testifies to the widespread nature of such confusion amongst British communists at the time.[33] Kapp has also described the immense relief she experienced in June 1941 when she could feel herself to be at one with her compatriots where the war was concerned.[34]

British Policy and the Refugees was completed in the spring of 1941, too soon to foresee this decisive turn in events. In fact, the release of the 'C' category internees was already well under way by then. Writing in 1988, François Lafitte chose to consider whether, with hindsight, the British internment and deportation of refugees from Nazi persecution in 1940 should be regarded as anything more than 'a trifling and short-lived episode', but concluded that 'this is not at all how we saw matters in the summer of 1940'. At that time, Lafitte continued, 'all who cherished democratic values were bound to feel uneasy, if not to protest'.[35]

Nor, clearly, are such concerns in any way outdated today. It seems most apposite that David Cesarani and Tony Kushner in their recent *The Internment of Aliens in Twentieth Century Britain*, which considers both First and Second World War alien internment policies, should conclude with a telling description of the detention and expulsion of Iraqis and others resident in Britain at the time of the 1991 Gulf War when the authorities once again indulged in 'a haphazard round up of "suspect" aliens guided by little more than prejudice and suspect information'.[36] As Cesarani and Kushner maintain:

> The tragedy of this episode was emphasized by the repetition, if on a smaller scale, of all the features and mistakes of the earlier internments. The detentions laid bare the marginality of non-citizens resident in the United Kingdom and the power as well as the prejudice of the security

> services. Mistakes were made – often as fundamental as detaining the wrong people – reflecting the inaccuracy, bias and redundancy of information on the basis of which bodies such as MI5 continue to operate. The episode showed the potential dangers facing democratic government if, as is now proposed, MI5 is given even greater powers in British society ... The detentions and other measures taken against 176 Iraqis and other Arabs (including seven Palestinians) also revealed the potential for abuse of British control procedures. More generally the sorry affair highlighted the dangers inherent in a country without a charter of individual rights, including the right to a fair trial or even *habeas corpus*.[37]

There is perhaps a certain satisfaction to be derived from the fact that in 1991, as in 1940, public opinion enjoyed a degree of success in contesting the measures against the detainees. Writing in 1993, however, Cesarani and Kushner assert that, despite this, state and society have not yet recognised 'the human misery, the abuse of power against innocents, the sheer waste of resources and, finally, the threat to democratic and accountable government that represents the true nature of alien internment in Britain'.[38] More than 50 years earlier, Yvonne Kapp and Margaret Mynatt were protesting in remarkably similar terms, on moral, economic and political grounds, against the British treatment of the refugees from Hitler. The moral case that they argue throughout, that the refugees, as 'the first victims of the Nazi regime in Germany, and the first fighters for its overthrow', should have been accorded a treatment very different from that currently being received, is of course self-evident. Economically, too, their position is indisputable: with reference to Norman Angell and Dorothy Buxton's prewar *You and the Refugee* – a work that had already pleaded strongly for the refugees to be regarded as an economic asset to Britain[39] – Kapp and Mynatt eloquently lament the waste of skill and labour to the British war effort resulting from the current refugee policies. And finally the case that Kapp and Mynatt advance is a political one, to the following effect: that, while for years the British people as a whole had allowed 'the right of asylum to be trampled on, the right to work to be denied, the right to a recognised status for our friends amongst the victims and opponents of Hitler to be ignored', these are rights, manifestly, 'which a democratic people ignores, denies and tramples on at its peril'. It is these ominous implications for British democracy that are stressed throughout Yvonne Kapp and Margaret Mynatt's devastating critique, and it is on this note, significantly, that the two authors choose to conclude their observations:

> In championing the cause of the refugees, we take a stand for our own democratic rights; in fighting for these we vindicate the refugees.

Charmian Brinson
Imperial College London
June 1996

NOTES

1. (London: Secker and Warburg, 1940), p. 250. Haffner completed his study in April 1940, following – ironically enough – his own first period of internment in Britain and preceding his second.
2. Under 'A London Diary', 9 March 1940, pp. 299–300. Bloomsbury House was in fact the home of the Jewish Refugees Committee.
3. G. Ward Price, 'There is More to be Done', *Daily Mail*, 24 May 1940, p. 4.
4. Beverley Nichols, 'I'd intern my German friends', *Sunday Chronicle*, 26 May 1940, p. 2.
5. On p. 5.
6. In *Reynolds News*, 28 July 1940, p. 6.
7. 'Judex', *Anderson's Prisoners* (London: Gollancz, 1940) (Victory Books No. 7).
8. François Lafitte, *The Internment of Aliens* (Harmondsworth: Penguin, 1940).
9. Lafitte, p. 181.
10. Yvonne Kapp, *Eleanor Marx*, Vol. I: *Family Life 1855–1883*; Vol. II: *The Crowded Years 1884–1898* (London: Lawrence & Wishart, 1972, 1976).
11. With Sally Alexander in Mary Chamberlain (ed.), *Writing Lives: Conversations between Women Writers* (London: Virago, 1988), pp. 100–17, with Mike Squires on 1 February and 21 July 1994, and with Charmian Brinson on 8 September 1994.
12. Alexander, p. 111.
13. From Yvonne Kapp, 'Time Will Tell' (unpublished MS.).
14. Ibid.
15. This account of Mynatt's biography is based on information from Yvonne Kapp (including from 'Time Will Tell'); the oration delivered by Eric Hobsbawm on the occasion of Mynatt's funeral, 1 March 1977, and the obituary he wrote for *The Times* (28 February 1977, p. 14); information from Nicholas Jacobs; and independent researches.
16. For a fuller account, see Charmian Brinson, *The Strange Case of Dora Fabian and Mathilde Wurm: A Study of German Political Exiles in London during the*

1930's (Berne: Lang, 1997), pp. 318–28. Mynatt's research formed the basis of Clara Leiser's (unpublished) article, 'Who Shared the Last Supper?'.

17. '"Die Seele" unserer ganzen Tätigkeit'; see Emmy Koenen, 'Erinnerungen: Zum antifaschistischen Kampf der KPD in der CSR', *Beiträge zur Geschichte der Arbeiterbewegung*, 18 (1976), p. 1067.
18. In Squires interview, 1 February 1994.
19. From 'Time Will Tell'.
20. In Brinson interview.
21. François Lafitte, 'Introduction: Afterthoughts Four Decades Later', in republished edition of *The Internment of Aliens* (London: Libris, 1988), p. xxi.
22. These include: Bernard Wasserstein, *Britain and the Jews of Europe 1939–1945* (London: Institute of Jewish Affairs/Oxford: Clarendon, 1979), pp. 81–108; Peter and Leni Gillman, *'Collar the Lot!': How Britain Interned and Expelled its Wartime Refugees* (London/Melbourne/New York: Quartet, 1980); Ronald Stent, *A Bespattered Page? The Internment of 'His Majesty's Most Loyal Enemy Aliens'* (London: Deutsch, 1980); Miriam Kochan, *Britain's Internees in the Second World War* (London/Basingstoke: Macmillan, 1983); Neil Stammers, *Civil Liberties in Britain during the Second World War: A Political Study* (London and Canberra: Croom Helm/New York: St Martin's Press, 1983), pp. 34–62; Michael Seyfert, *Deutsche Exilliteratur in britischer Internierung: Ein unbekanntes Kapitel der Kulturgeschichte des Zweiten Weltkriegs* (Berlin: Arsenal, 1984); Michael Seyfert, 'His Majesty's Most Loyal Internees', in Gerhard Hirschfeld (ed.), *Exile in Great Britain: Refugees from Hitler's Germany* (Leamington Spa: Berg/Atlantic Highlands, NJ: Humanities Press, 1984), pp. 163–94; Connery Chappell, *Island of Barbed Wire: Internment on the Isle of Man in World War Two* (London: Hale, 1984); David Cesarani and Tony Kushner (eds), *The Internment of Aliens in Twentieth Century Britain* (London: Cass, 1993).
23. Hans Jaeger, 'Refugees' Internment in Britain 1939–40: A Survey of Literature', *Wiener Library Bulletin*, 9, Nos 3–4 (May–August 1955), p. 31.
24. Paul Hoch, 'Gaoling the victim', *Immigrants and Minorities*, 4, No. 1 (March 1985), p. 81.
25. For a later, if rather different analysis of this area, see Tony Kushner's 'Clubland, Cricket Tests and Alien Internment, 1939–40', in Cesarani and Kushner (eds), pp. 79–101.
26. Hoch, p. 81.
27. On p. 97. 'Scipio's' *100,000,000 Allies – If We Choose* appeared in 1940 as No. 2 in Gollancz's Victory Books series.
28. In his (unpublished) review of Hirschfeld (ed.), *Exile in Great Britain: Refugees from Hitler's Germany.*
29. Squires interview, 1 February 1994.
30. Letter from Tony Kushner to the present writer, 15 December 1994.
31. From 'Time Will Tell'.
32. For instance, in Squires interview, 21 July 1994.
33. For a detailed discussion of the communist dilemma at this time, see for example Kevin Morgan, *Against Fascism and War: Ruptures and Continuities in British Communist Politics 1935–41* (Manchester: Manchester University Press, 1989).

34. Squires interview, 21 July 1994.
35. Lafitte (1988), pp. vii–ix.
36. Cesarani and Kushner, p. 215.
37. Ibid., p. 214.
38. Ibid., p. 215.
39. Norman Angell and Dorothy Frances Buxton, *You and the Refugee: the Morals and Economics of the Problem* (Harmondsworth: Penguin, 1939).

1968 Foreword

British Policy and the Refugees, never published, was written in Howtown, Ullswater, between June and October 1940. Certain slight additions were made, to bring it up to date, in the spring of 1941 during negotiations in London with a publisher.

The date of its writing is important for a proper understanding of the book; students making use of the material should be aware of the political situation behind this study of the refugees in Britain. Indeed, such historical value as it has lies in the fact that it was not written with hindsight – when the problems it deals with had been resolved by later events – but at the moment when the role and the fate of refugees in this country were a burning issue.

The two British authors had held, until May 1940, responsible positions[1] in the British refugee relief organisation which had played the leading part in bringing political refugees to Britain – including large numbers of German, Austrian and Czechoslovak Communists – and in providing for their maintenance and care. In May 1940 both the authors were summarily dismissed from their posts by the Home Office on account of their political affiliations. This apparently isolated instance of victimisation was subsequently seen to be merely a prelude to the wholesale arrest of the refugees themselves.

This was the period of the Nazi occupation of France and the Low Countries when the invasion of Britain was daily expected and genuinely feared. The German–Soviet Non-Aggression Pact was still in force and persons suspected of sympathy with the Soviet Union were regarded as a potential danger to Britain.

It was also a period when the war aims of the Allies were undefined and dubious. Many influential groups, both within and outside government circles, had hoped from the outbreak of war that the Wehrmacht would fulfil its 'historic mission' as a 'bulwark against Communism' and, after the defeat of Poland, continue its eastward march to destroy the Soviet Union. The capitulation of Pétain's France demonstrated the strength of the forces of reaction in the West. Their hopes of 'switching the war' to the East were by no means abandoned.

In this situation the defenceless and dependent refugees in Britain could have been exploited to serve reactionary ends.

Nobody truly concerned with their welfare believed that in wartime they alone, of the entire population, could remain 'above the battle', pursuing their émigré politics (on government maintenance grants) and in no way involved in the war effort of the British people. It was clearly foreseen from the start that four, and only four, possibilities would be open to them: they could become part of the civilian labour force (working in factories, shipyards, mines, forestry, agriculture and so forth); they could be conscripted into the armed services; they could be used by the government, the press and the radio for propaganda purposes on a large scale (even though war aims were undeclared); or they could be imprisoned.

The authors of this book in their official capacity, realising that these were, indeed, the only possibilities, recommended the first course (namely, civilian employment) and worked out the practical measures to implement it. It became the adopted policy, which operated until June 1940. It is worth remarking that such notable German members of the English emigration as Wilhelm Koenen quickly grasped the necessity of this approach and its full political implications.

To understand the internal British situation at that juncture it must be recalled that it was the position not only of political refugees but also of British Communists and Communist sympathisers which was in jeopardy, culminating in the banning of the *Daily Worker* in January 1941, by which time many leading Party officials had gone into factories and were working at their former trades.

With the Nazi attack on the Soviet Union in June 1941 the political situation was entirely transformed – though it may be noted that, despite the change of political climate, the ban on the *Daily Worker* was not lifted until August 1942.

British Policy and the Refugees was accepted by a leading publisher, but while negotiations were still in progress a popular volume on the subject, of a very different political complexion, appeared in paperback.[2] It was thought to meet the demand for any book on refugees and the proposal to publish the present work was dropped.

At some stage, the date now forgotten, the material was lent (in effect, given) to a friend in East Germany writing reminiscences of exile in Britain.

Since then, the one copy of the MS in the authors' possession has remained untouched and unread for nearly 30 years. It emerged from oblivion only when other British comrades, engaged in writing a social history of the 1930s, asked for information about refugee policy in that period. On re-reading the MS themselves the authors realised that with the passage of time – and despite its polemical character – the material had become of some historical interest to generations who have grown up in the years since the defeat of Hitler and, perhaps in particular, to those in the 'refugee-producing' countries of the Hitler era.

Y.K.
M.M.
London
May 1968

NOTES

1. The one as Assistant to the Director of the Czech Refugee Trust Fund and Secretary to the Trustees; the other as head of the Tribunals Department in the same government-sponsored organisation.
2. François Lafitte, *The Internment of Aliens* (Harmondsworth: Penguin 1940). (The author was Henry Havelock Ellis's stepson.)

Introduction

This book is an attempt to show the present treatment of the refugees from Nazi oppression in the context of their history as refugees in Britain.

While they have had their forthright champions both amongst Members of Parliament and independent authorities, their tireless and devoted friends in the refugee organisations and amongst large sections of the British public, and their spokesmen in the press, the wrongs the refugees suffer today have a deeper meaning than can usefully be expressed in the heat of battle for the restoration of the elementary rights of these men and women.

Already a vast literature of pamphlets, articles, reports and speeches has accumulated since the mass-internment policy was introduced by the government on 21 June 1940. Many and excellent words have been spoken and written in recent months to demonstrate how vital to the war effort are the services of the anti-Nazi refugees who now rot in the internment camps.

Inhumane policies do not spring from nowhere and this book tries to explain both the origins of these policies and the wider purpose of the refugees. As long as these men and women are not at freedom, whether they are in concentration camps in Germany, Austria, Czechoslovakia, or in internment camps in France or Britain makes no difference: there can be no freedom for the peoples of Europe. The refugees are an index of our war and peace aims.

In this brief account of British policy and the refugees in the past, as well as the present, we have done no more than compile the facts and place them in their true perspective.

That the lessons these facts teach have not been learned yet is our justification for this book.

Y.K.
M.M.
October 1940

'Definition:

a) Persons possessing or having possessed German nationality and not possessing any other nationality who are proved not to enjoy, in law or in fact, the protection of the German Government.

b) Stateless persons not covered by previous Conventions or Agreements who have left German territory after being established therein and who are proved not to enjoy, in law or in fact, the protection of the German Government.'

Convention concerning the Status of Refugees coming from Germany
Geneva, 10 February 1938.

Part One
THE REFUGEE ERA

Exodus

Who and what the refugees are – Why and how they fled – Regulations governing entry and sojourn

1

Between the years 1933–39 the United Kingdom received some 80,000 to 90,000 refugees from countries under Nazi rule. Some 20,000 to 30,000 of these re-emigrated before the outbreak of war.

Today, when everyone remotely interested in the subject is familiar with the conception of, on the one side, 'racial' and, on the other, 'political' refugees, the precise nature of the elements that went to make up this considerable immigration is either unknown or forgotten. In the debates in Parliament, as in public speeches and private conversations, the figure of the refugee is variously represented, according to the experience of the speaker, as a helpless, wretched and pathetic victim; a militant, fearless and unbroken fighter; or a dangerous spy wearing the most treacherous of all masks to win the confidence and sympathy of a humane people. The holders of these views accuse each other of a lack of realism: each sees the other's conception as a sentimental or alarmist fiction and can cite incidents and cases to support their own view. Each would grant that there are exceptions to the general run of victims (or fighters, or spies), and that these could and should be singled out and accorded treatment different from that advocated for the mass, but beyond this concession to the probability that 60,000 persons are not all of the same kind, our legislators, like many of our public speakers and our friends, show a singular disregard for the facts and for the necessity to examine them with care, preferring, like bad novelists, to depict their characters in strong, unconvincing colours: black or white.

No research is needed to establish beyond doubt that the approximately 60,000 refugees from Germany, Austria and Czechoslovakia who found themselves in Britain at the outbreak of war were of all shades; and some, to the undoing of simple-minded people, of many. All that is needed is a cursory glance at the history of the refugee era and a little common-sense.

Who were the persons attacked, persecuted and dispossessed on Hitler's accession to power?

There were the victims of the terror which began during the night of the Reichstag fire. The leaders and prominent members of the Communist Party, as well as many other left-wing politicians and intellectuals, were killed, imprisoned and driven into illegality or exile. 'By the end of May 1933 the Communist Party was practically outlawed, most of its leaders having been killed, imprisoned, or having fled, and the rank and file driven from employment.'[1]

There were the Social Democrats, Trade Unionists, Liberals and Pacifists, whose organisations had been outlawed and whose leaders had been killed, arrested or driven into exile by the summer of 1933, when all parties except the National Socialist (Nazi) Party became illegal. 'It was not until the Communists were disposed of that the attack on the Social Democrats and the "free" trade unions began in earnest, although some Social Democrat leaders had been taken into protective custody and some trade-union buildings had been occupied early in March.'[2]

There were the civil servants, lawyers, doctors, writers, artists, actors and booksellers who were banned from the ordinary practice of their profession by the Non-Aryan laws succeeding the National Boycott Day of 1 April 1933.

There was the attack on Jewish shopkeepers and private traders which was intensified in 1934, culminating in the second wave of Jewish persecution legalised by the Nuremberg laws of September 1935, which banned Jewish employees.

There was the persecution of the Confessional Church, which gathered momentum in 1934.

There were the dissident Nazi leaders and erstwhile collaborators who, if they were not killed, had been driven into exile after 30 June 1934 (the 'Night of the Long Knives').

There were the German Nationalists (Conservatives) and old 'Front Fighters' who were eliminated from the State machinery.

There were the opponents of Hitler from the Saar, forced to flee after the Plebiscite of January 1935.

There were the big Jewish industrialists and bankers who, insofar as they had not left Germany before, were forced out of business in 1937–38.

There were the political and racial victims of the same, but more rapid process in Austria from March 1938.

There was the persecution of Catholics, given open expression in the attacks on the Church in 1938, and carried through in Germany and Austria with increasing zeal after this date.

There was the entire anti-Henlein opposition in the 'Sudeten' areas of Czechoslovakia, exposed by the Munich Agreement to ruthless persecution.

There were the last and most numerous victims of the Jewish pogroms in Germany which followed the assassination of Vom Rath in Paris in November 1938.

There were the fugitives from all these earlier persecutions who had found asylum in Czechoslovakia and whose extradition was demanded by the German government between October 1938 and March 1939.

Finally, adding their terrible urgency to that of the hundreds of thousands of men, women and children seeking to emigrate from Germany, Austria and the Sudeten areas where they were excluded from citizen rights, there were the political and racial refugees who fled after the Nazi occupation of the rest of Czechoslovakia in March 1939.

Throughout the Nazi era, there were those who, not excluded by previous laws and persecution, became endangered owing to their active opposition to Hitler, which these laws and this persecution bred, and at the other end of the scale those German, Austrian and Czechoslovak nationals who, although not in any way directly threatened, found personal life and business dealings irksome under the Nazi regime and preferred to live elsewhere, to which category must be added the cultured liberals who were repelled by the education in barbarism which alone was offered to their children.

On the one hand, then, there were the pitiable, tormented Jews, many of whom were so politically innocent that they regarded the inescapable fate that had overtaken them as a purely individual tragedy; on the other, the Socialists, Communists, Trade Unionists, members of the active Protestant and Catholic opposition, of the democratic peace and cultural movements and of the co-operatives, who scorned to make the compromises open to them and paid for their convictions with death, imprisonment, torture and exile.

Between these two major categories – the victims pure and simple, and the open opponents, many of whom were also Jews – there lay the little shadow-world of renegades from Left and Right; of disappointed Nazi careerists and coalitionists; of fascist adventurers, unsuccessful at home; of intriguers with small and ugly political axes to grind (and who found ready whetstones amongst the influential backstairs politicians of this and other countries); of professional spies from Central Europe who, during a period rife with opportunity, frequently changed or multiplied their employers; and, both last and least, the small residuum of paid and unpaid Gestapo agents masquerading as refugees, amongst whom must be counted the despicable but tragic wrecks, broken by concentration camps, who were released on the promise to work for their persecutors. This heterogeneous collection of shadow men and women, whose histories in many cases are not clear, since they have much to hide, provides first-class material for second-rate drama; from it many excellent morals might be drawn to adorn a speech in the House; it lends itself, indeed, to a variety of purposes, but not, it would be thought, to forming the basis of a policy. There are very good reasons for thinking this.

The uninformed belief that spies and agents could pose as refugees and hoodwink the public with the greatest of ease is contradicted by the facts.[3] In the first place there is a very firm consensus of opinion concerning their fellows amongst the refugees themselves.

No group has had more to lose by tolerating shady characters in its midst than this community of exiles. Genuine refugees from Nazi oppression could never condone or view with complacency the presence of Hitler's agents. Such an attitude would be suicidal. It has to be remembered not only that the refugees include political opponents of the Nazis who have a price on their heads; that instances of political murder in exile and of kidnapping with intent to murder are not unknown; that every element despised by the Hitler regime is represented among the refugees, and also that great numbers of the refugees fled leaving behind wives or husbands, parents, children and friends, many of whom are to this day in the slaughterhouses known as concentration camps.

Such men and women have motives as deep and compelling as any moving a government department to discourage the undesirable elements amongst refugees. The political convictions of the genuine anti-fascists, of which their victimisation gives evidence, reinforced by the most intense personal interests, make it imperative that every dubious character should be scrutinised and eliminated from their company. They can only wish today that the Home Office had taken prompt and drastic action against these characters at the start.

While having the best of all reasons for exposing suspicious individuals, the refugees also have the best information on which to base their suspicions. The histories of many of the shadow men and women amongst the refugees are not clear but their activities in recent years, their contacts in Germany and, above all, the circumstances surrounding their emigration, are known to at least some section of the *bona fide* exiles, whose own safety demanded a very close watch on precisely these matters.

To the British public at large, the refugees are an assortment of foreigners comprising every type of alien from the enemy country. There may be very strong sympathy in Britain for the victims of the bestiality and tyranny of the Nazis but they remain foreigners in our eyes and we do not credit them at first blush with exercising the same discrimination that we would automatically apply amongst ourselves (on the analogy that many Europeans cannot see the difference between one Chinese face and another, and are inclined to believe that the Chinese cannot do so either).

Let the British reader picture himself in a foreign land, with a host of his compatriots, in circumstances where his good faith and his good conduct are the conditions of his freedom and safety. Be he a former Member of Parliament, a Trade Union leader, an active Socialist, an honest professional man, or simply a decent, obscure citizen, he will bring with him a shrewd knowledge of his fellow-countrymen in his own sphere and district and will view with alarm the inclusion in this band of exiles of any person whose character or antecedents are liable to bring disaster or discredit upon the community. Suppose your company of exiles was drawn from all regions of the British Isles and from most sections of the population, with a large admixture of people who had taken part in some organised form of political, social, religious or professional life. If an entirely unknown Englishman suddenly turned up in emigration and announced that he had been a member of the Bromley Labour Party, or secretary of the Glasgow Jewish Board of Guardians, or the Medical Officer of Health for Wythenshawe, is it not probable that the Bromley or the Glasgow or the Wythenshawe people would have something to say about this and would regard with more than common mistrust a person representing himself to be something they knew he quite certainly was not? Would they not also immediately warn the officials of the organisation to whom the impostor applied for help?

Or again, suppose yourself confronted in this emigration by a person who does not misrepresent himself but whom you have reason to doubt: perhaps a man known throughout long years of uneasy association; a person met once or twice in suspicious circumstances; a person whose reputation in your town has always been equivocal; or, on the other hand, a person so notoriously untrustworthy that he could only have passed himself off as a legitimate émigré by guile and underhand influence. In every case you would be fearfully on your guard. Add to this the perpetual dread that, if not your own life, then that of your family at home in Britain could be jeopardised by the activities of these uncertain elements, and you will understand why refugees whose own integrity is beyond doubt treat with the greatest wariness even those of their formerly reliable colleagues whose history, since they fell into the hands of the Gestapo, is not fully known, and shun like the plague those others who, however they may have presented their cases to obtain admission to this country, had an unsavoury reputation at home.

Nor must it be thought that the refugee organisations were staffed by gullible fools. Even without the refugees' own very significant reactions to their fellows, there were ways in which the 'bad hat' revealed himself quite unmistakably in the course of weekly contacts and voluminous correspondence with persons trained in social work or versed in international politics and human affairs. A 'wrong' type of refugee quite often gave himself away by the very manner of his appeals for help; he marked himself out by a display of interest in matters not legitimately the concern of refugees at all; and it was quite impossible for him to live in a fashion, or on means, or enjoy privileges not ordinarily available to refugees without the facts being known and recorded, in the course of the administrative routine, by the refugee workers. The *dossiers* of each case were not intended to serve as character case-histories – such researches were left to the higher authorities – but it was inevitable that the basic formal data (giving times and places of birth, of residence, date of emigration and reason for emigration, supplemented by the vast correspondence with or about the refugee, with his friends, his landlady, his local committee throughout his whole sojourn in this country and preceding it) should have presented a very clear picture of the individual's character and purposes, laying bare any discrepancies in his self-portrait, any anomalies in his story.

It has been argued that it would have been simple enough for those 'refugees' who wished to escape notice and were furnished by the Gestapo with forged documents and credentials to avoid detection by assuming the refugee personality in every particular. Apart from the safeguards provided by the vigilance of the refugees (who have a highly developed nose for the scent of the Gestapo), it must be remembered that the refugee's life was a very circumscribed one and that in the majority of cases it entailed an almost total dependence upon a refugee organisation. To be a refugee meant to live that life: to be in perpetual contact with a certain number of refugee workers whose experience of thousands of cases, even without exercising special alertness, would detect any divergence from the usual demands or activities of refugees. It meant that every detail, from unexplained journeys to new clothes, had to be accounted for, not primarily to allay suspicion, but because government funds, or funds contributed by the charitable public, were dispensed. If, moreover, to evade this niggling control, the impostor had been smuggled in as a 'private' case, on the financial guarantee and under the personal charge of an individual settled (with a bank balance) in this country, then the credentials of that individual had been scrutinised by the organisation through whom the application was made, or by the Home Office itself if the application was made directly, and the sponsor himself was unlikely to have undertaken the unlimited liability such guarantees represented unless he was either personally acquainted with the refugee and his circumstances (and could vouch for his character) or was consciously lending himself to Nazi purposes; a quite possible contingency, but one that would involve other connections and activities in this country which should not have escaped the knowledge and notice of the appropriate authorities.

There were two categories who could avoid contacts with refugees and refugee organisations and the automatic control such contacts exercised: the rich 'non-Aryans' whose own money, rather than that of some guarantor in this country, obtained for them the right of asylum and independence of movement, and the domestic servants brought to this country on Ministry of Labour permits, who might or might not be sufferers from Nazi oppression and who had no need either to mix with other refugees or to frequent the offices of the refugee organisations. These two categories suffered relatively less than the general run of refugees in the internment round-up.

There was another very good reason against the Nazi agent choosing the role of refugee: before the war, it was easier for German nationals to enter this country under any and every other guise. Provided they had money, they did so with the greatest frequency and facility as tourists, commercial travellers, businessmen and journalists.

It was therefore quite plain (and was recognised by the refugees and their protectors, the refugee organisations) that the task allotted to the 'refugee' Nazi agent was solely that of spying upon the refugees themselves. Not for them, in the course of apparently legitimate business, the interviews with industrial or government experts, the freedom of movement throughout the length and breadth of the country, the access, without arousing the suspicion of the British authorities, to the German Embassy and Consulates. Instead they experienced the frugal, often communal life of the dependent exile, without privacy, privilege or status. Not everyone's cup of tea.

Many of the arguments against accepting and treating the refugees as decent human beings rest on the absurd assumption that the genuine and tragic refugee from Nazi oppression does not exist at all. Once it is admitted that such people do exist and that their credentials have been examined, then the only tenable position is to recognise them for what they are: the first victims of the Nazi régime in Germany and the first fighters for its overthrow.

Let us now hear Mr Peake the Parliamentary Under-Secretary for Home Affairs and spokesman for the Department responsible for refugee policy:

> Practically all the aliens who have come to this country in the last five or six years have been sponsored either by a refugee organisation or by

> a private individual ... Apart from that vouching of character by the organisation or the individual, there was then an examination by the British Consul abroad of the *bona fides* of the individuals who wished to come. Then there was a scrutiny by the immigration officer when the alien came to this country. After landing, the alien had to report and register with the local police, and since the outbreak of the war every German and Austrian has been before a tribunal of some kind or another; many of them have been before two tribunals ... I can only say, on behalf of the Home Secretary and myself, that I wish we knew half as much about many of the neutral aliens and many British subjects as we know about the enemy aliens now in this country ...[4]

The plea that 'it is humanly impossible to devise a completely satisfactory method of searching human hearts', advanced at a later date by Mr Herbert Morrison[5] to maintain a policy of continued internment, strikes a note oddly out of harmony with Mr Peake's frank exposition of the methods that it had been humanly possible to devise.

That a section of suspects would exist and might in time of emergency become not merely a potential risk but a very real menace was a foregone conclusion and one that must have been reached many years ago by the responsible authorities. It was a conclusion inherent in granting immigration to the assorted types of people seeking sanctuary during the past years: Jews, Socialists, Catholics and Conservatives, Trade Unionists, Communists, Monarchists and old 'Front Fighters', Protestants, Pacifists and Hitler's discomfited rivals. The types are many, but there is not a single individual amongst them of whom the Home Office, the police, the Tribunal Presidents, the immigration authorities, the refugee organisations and the large body of reliable refugees themselves could not, between them, give a comprehensive account. It would indeed be contemptible if any general refugee policy had been based on the alleged inability of the government to distinguish between friends and foes.

A very different inability underlies the policy adopted in May 1940, and none knows it better than the permanent officials of the Home Office, through whose hands have passed, for seven years, the papers of aliens seeking admission to this country.

Here is an example given by a government spokesman of the kind of official justification for interning 30,000 victimised and destitute Jews, Communists, Liberals, Socialists, Trade Unionists:

> May I instance a case which arose in South Africa? A German who had been for many years in South Africa was a very important member of the Government. He was employed by an insurance company and was a director of that company until he joined the South African Government. This German had no contact with other Germans in Capetown. He did not belong to their clubs or institutions. His social life was spent entirely among the British community. He played golf, cricket and so forth, and everyone of the directors of his company was so confident of his good faith that without exception they petitioned to secure his immediate release. In that particular case papers in the possession of the police proved beyond doubt that he was a most dangerous man, the pivotal man of the German Government ...[6]

The point made by Mr Peake and the Duke of Devonshire, both speaking on behalf of the government, amounts to this: the credentials of the majority of refugees, as a body, are known and above suspicion, but certain well-placed individuals, whom it is not at all pleasant to suspect, may be acting as Hitler's agents.

The latter fact will, of course, only surprise and impress the naïve. Nobody else would dream of looking for 'pivotal men of the German Government' amongst its hounded and ruined victims, even though it is admitted that these might include Gestapo spies planted to watch the German opposition elements in exile. The absurdity of supposing that the German Secret Service would recruit its members for work in Britain from amongst those who could not speak English has been pointed out;[7] also, there was not the smallest need to resort to so clumsy a device considering the number of well-spoken and even cricketing Fascists who enjoyed the confidence of British society.

2

The British reader has been asked to project himself into the situation of the exile abroad. It would be quite impossible for him to make a similar identification with the refugee before flight: the conditions are lacking in his experience. An Englishman cannot even picture himself in the material and psychological circumstances of the majority of those who eventually sought safety in Britain. He does not know what it means to be afraid of opening one's mouth in the presence of one's workmates, in shops, in bars, even at home. He cannot understand how it feels when the man with whom one has worked side-by-side for years, or one's next-door neighbour, or the familiar face behind the counter, suddenly disappears, never to be heard of again by a distracted family, while unidentifiable remains, sinister beyond words, are thrown into the mortuary or an official calls to say that they can have the ashes on payment of a small sum. No Englishman can understand this unless he is a criminal who waits nightly for the death-warrant which a knock at the door may mean. Nor do elderly men expect to be dragged from their beds and trampled under jackboots because they have worshipped God according to their fathers' teachings. Men and women were denounced by their children; spied on by their colleagues, pitting their honesty and courage against the vast unscrupulous machine of the secret police with its huge arsenal of weapons of torture, and finally, when the mental anxiety had reached its height, subjected to physical maltreatment: teeth bashed in, feet crushed to pulp, ribs broken and faces slashed – no, the Englishman cannot think himself into the position of the refugees before they came here.

He can, however, very well appreciate the urgency of the need to escape and will marvel at the strength of character of those Germans who, notwithstanding the dangers and the tortures they underwent, chose to remain in their country until death itself was the only alternative to flight. This was the role of those who stayed to carry on the work of the illegal opposition to Hitler, to smuggle leaflets into the factory or office, to reorganise in secret the smashed Trade Unions, to speak forbidden words against Nazi war preparations, to collect money for the pariah families of the men in concentration camps and to stir the mute and latent anger of those who contributed to such funds.

It is plain that when at last such men and women could no longer hold out against the certain consequences of their actions and had to fly or die in circumstances of peculiarly horrible agony, as so many of their fellows had already done, their emigration was not elaborately organised. No exchange of letters with aid committees, documented life-histories and well-arranged future plans preceded their arrival in this or other countries of asylum. Incidentally, few of them sought refuge in the United Kingdom immediately, preferring places such as Czechoslovakia, France, Holland, Switzerland or the Scandinavian countries whose borders were contiguous with Germany. Some of these countries also allowed the émigrés to continue their political life as anti-Nazis.

This category of refugees, of whom we entertained a few thousand in Great Britain (prior to their transportation in June and July 1940), had little in common in the manner of their emigration from the Nazi countries with the so-called ordered and controlled exodus of the majority of 'racial' and 'economic' refugees.

It is known that while Jews, for no other reason than that they were Jews (or half-Jews, or quarter-Jews) were hunted and tortured by the Gestapo, one of their chief functions was to yield spoil. (The other was to provide sport for the athletes of the SS.) While the politically active anti-Nazi was a 'wanted' man in the police sense, the Jews were 'unwanted' economically. This is not the place to describe at length the role of the Jew as scapegoat – it has in any case been done admirably by George Sacks in *The Intelligent Man's Guide to Jew-Baiting* (London, 1935), and the plight of the Jews in Germany has been described by Louis Golding in *The Jewish Problem* (Harmondsworth, 1938) – but it is necessary to refer here to the two main by-products of Nazi anti-Semitism: dispossession and confiscation.

To replace Jews outstanding in the learned, scientific and liberal professions – where they have always excelled since they were admitted – by Nazi mediocrities it was necessary to be rid, once and for all, of these inconveniently eminent rivals. One may present a Jewish professor or scientist as an obscene criminal to the public at large but it is difficult to persuade his associates and pupils of this view: he must be liquidated altogether.

On the other hand even small Jewish businessmen collectively represented a tidy sum of money, which could be lifted from them as the price of escape from conditions which were daily made more humiliating and unbearable. The same applied to the large body of middling professional people – Jewish lawyers and doctors with flourishing practices; teachers, journalists and civil servants with good salaries – whose elimination, in common with that of the distinguished figures in the academic and artistic world, left room for the Nazi second-raters to snatch their places.

The emigration, then, of these classes was 'facilitated'. This does not mean that it was made easy or pleasant: weeks had to be spent producing accounts of income and property for the purposes of confiscation, which was in effect licensed robbery; weeks more passed in lining up outside the various passport and police offices for papers, these activities being sometimes interrupted by arrest and a spell of internment, with all its hideous concomitants, on trumped-up charges of currency-smuggling or professional malpractice – or on no charge at all – and then came the mortifying process of going, hat-in-hand, to one's former university or other place of employment, to beg for a copy of a diploma or testimonial and to be called a filthy Jew and left standing, once, twice, three times, before the document – on which was pinned the hope of any future – was finally, and with fresh insults, produced.

During this period of hateful and protracted negotiations for exit permits, the Jews were further subjected to the agony of watching their children's lives being deformed by hatred and cruelty. To normal parents this was perhaps the most crushing grief and certainly one that made the need for escape desirable beyond all other considerations. The Nazis knew this well and stiffened the cash terms in accordance.

It should not be thought that the entire population joined in Jew-baiting. Some sections dissociated themselves from official anti-Semitism and even opened their purses and their homes to the wretched and dispossessed Jews of their acquaintance, at great risk to themselves.

In Britain, as wave upon wave of Jewish refugees succeeded each pogrom and each tightening of the anti-Jewish laws, the refugee aid organisations, already working at top pressure, found themselves almost unable to cope with the flood of applications. Inevitable bottlenecks occurred in trying to canalise this irresistible tide of human need into the narrowly framed immigration regulations, with the result that to the callous procrastinations and deliberate hindrances imposed by the Nazis at one end were added intolerable delays at the other. Letters would lie unanswered, forms unfilled, applications unfiled, while the impatient and agonised human being abroad touched ever lower depths of despair.

The refugee aid committees were in no sense to blame. Voluntarily and single-handed, against the odds of a fundamentally ungenerous Aliens Order and restrictive regulations, they carried out the noble task of rescuing and relieving the persecuted thousands.

Letters reached them from almost every well-intentioned person in the British Isles who knew or had even a remote interest in some unhappy German Jew. There were offers of unlimited guarantees of support – and one cannot too greatly admire the spirit of their writers – from people who had once, on some long-ago holiday in Switzerland, encountered a little provincial Jewish doctor or lawyer for a few weeks, who now, clinging to this frail thread, his sole 'connection' with an Englishman, had pleaded for help. Such offers had to be examined and sometimes rejected; this did not prevent the potential guarantor persisting in his offer and increasing the volume of correspondence. There were peremptory letters from persons with more influence than knowledge of the regulations and critical letters from persons with more money than patience; there were letters from every Jewish, liberal and anti-Nazi organisation in the country; and, finally, there were the letters, with diplomas and certificates and affidavits and photographs and testimonials and autobiographies and press-cuttings from the potential refugees themselves. The department dealing with doctors and dentists was in correspondence with over 6,000 individuals in these professions alone. On average every refugee wrote to the organisation once a week prior to his emigration, and almost every case had its attendant coterie of letter-writers and callers among British friends and sympathisers.

By 1938, with the annexation of Austria and the renewed pogroms in Germany, the task of the voluntary organisations became so onerous that nothing short of a complete administrative reorganisation (which is precisely what the stress of the moment forbade) could have turned the multiple *ad hoc* committees and departments bred of expediency into an efficient service. What they did was magnificent, but the problem was beyond the power of private enterprise to solve, as Mr James McDonald had discovered and recorded before relinquishing his office as High Commissioner for Refugees as far back as January 1936.[8]

No one who visited the offices of the main refugee committees at that time will ever forget the daily scene. Before one had turned the corner of the street the waiting throng of refugees standing close-packed on the pavements and in the roadways was enough to arouse whatever anti-Semitism – or anti-fascism – was latent in the onlooker. One had to fight to push one's way in at the door and then, still shoved and jostled, one was in the enormous room where in stolid though not quiet assembly the multitude of desperate petitioners stood waiting – for news, for help, for advice, for something, anything, that would enable them to return to their miserable quarters with hope refreshed. Later benches were placed in this hall and then, like some nightmare out-patients department for the incurable, the refugees would sit for hours on end in humble, tragic rows, waiting and hoping. In Germany or Austria the relatives of these sad figures, for whom they waited and hoped, would find themselves at long last stripped of their worldly possessions and, with the loathsome formalities behind them, with an exit permit valid for a limited period – and no news from England. Then they would hurry to Consulate and Passport Control officials, rush home again for letters, line up in fresh queues, beg for further interviews with the authorities and, before this feverish activity had spent itself, the permit had lapsed, the concentration camp yawned once more and, if life and health were spared, all was to be done again. In many cases suicide presented itself as the easier way out.

These, then, were the 'facilitated' emigrations.

The political refugees made their escape under conditions that were just as fraught with difficulty and anxiety, but without the possibility of obtaining emigration papers, without the solace of correspondence with refugee organisations abroad and often spending each hunted night in a different place. They crossed frontiers illegally; they left without papers or with borrowed papers and in disguise; they went without knowing whether they would ever see their families again or indeed without knowing their families' whereabouts. For most of these refugees there was no promise of a family reunion if they reached safety; there were no comfortable guarantors awaiting them; they were not men who, through family ties or social connections, foreign travel, business or professional association could claim friends abroad. Such connections that they had were of a political character and the main refugee organisations were not among them.

This requires a word of explanation, since it is obvious that both the public and the authorities were fully aware of political, as distinct from racial, persecution by the Nazis and that it claimed more martyrs and at least as many victims.[9] The drive against them had been swifter and more ruthless, and the numbers were larger. In the

German Reichstag election of 5 March 1933, and despite the wholesale terror let loose after the Reichstag fire, 11,877,615 men and women cast their votes for the Socialist and Communist Parties; the number of Jews in Germany was below 600,000.[10] It is a fact, however, that the most important refugee aid committees, which alone could draw on large sums of money and were *personae gratae* with the authorities, were not set up for the saving of Socialists, Communists and Trade Unionists. They had the explicit function of dealing with the problem of the racial refugees – large enough in all conscience – and it was not until the events of 1938 shook the British public to its depths and rudely awakened it to its special obligations as a democratic country that the rescue of political refugees was recognised as a legitimate undertaking. Even then this work remained chiefly in the hands of the British Committee for Refugees from Czechoslovakia, the post-Munich organisation set up for the purpose of bringing out refugees from the ceded Sudeten areas and the rest of Czechoslovakia.

Immediately after the cession of the Sudeten areas to Germany, Sudeten German and Czech anti-fascists (known in their localities for their public stand against Henlein) – Socialists, Communists, Trade Unionists, Co-operators, Liberals, writers, publicists, town councillors and mayors, leaders and members of the voluntary defence militias who had actively participated in the suppression of the Henlein *putsch* shortly before the cession – fled in their tens of thousands to Czech territory. They swelled the numbers – also in their thousands – of the fugitives from Germany and Austria who had already taken refuge there.

The Czechoslovak government was unable and unwilling to cope with this new influx of refugees and stated that in no circumstances could any but the Czechs and Slovaks remain in Czechoslovakia. Having lost many of its industries by the cession of territory and finding its entire economic life disrupted, the country was not in a position to provide homes and work for this destitute mass; moreover, it would have meant the creation of a new German minority, which the Czechoslovak government would not tolerate. The governments of Great Britain and France were therefore informed that unless the refugees from the Sudeten areas, as well as from Germany and Austria, were allowed to emigrate speedily, they would be sent back to German territory. The German government, having long before prepared lists of political opponents who had so far escaped their clutches, now insisted on their extradition from Czechoslovakia. The government of betrayed and mutilated Czechoslovakia was hardly in a position to refuse this demand for long, and while in some cases political refugees from Germany were extradited and immediately executed, thousands of refugees from the Sudeten territory were driven back by the gendarmes to those areas where imprisonment, torture and death awaited them.

Both the British and French governments were reluctant to admit the victims of their diplomacy. In October 1938, under great pressure, the British government granted 350 block visas[11] – 250 for Sudeten refugees and 100 for German and Austrian refugees – and then the scramble for transport began.

Not one of the refugees whose extradition had been demanded by the Nazis was able to travel through Germany. Poland allowed only holders of valid Czechoslovak passports to travel through its territory. The Germans and Austrians, however, as well as many of the Sudeten Germans, had nothing but Czech Interim passports (a kind of refugee travelling certificate). The only way for these, then, was to fly over Germany and take the long chance of a forced landing on German soil with all its consequences. There were, however, only two planes a day that were not scheduled to land in Germany: one to Holland and one to France. It was impossible to put on extra planes as this entailed obtaining the consent of the German government. Only a few refugees could therefore be transported every day; on some days none at all. The whole procedure represented a terrible drain on the funds of the voluntary bodies responsible for the rescue work.

Meanwhile the British Committee for Refugees from Czechoslovakia, the High Commissioner for Refugees, an important section of Members of Parliament and the press urged that more visas should be granted. After great delays the government consented and another hundred block visas were issued to Germans and Austrians. Thereafter, between January and March 1939, a further steady, if thin, trickle of block visas filtered through to Czechoslovakia. The transport difficulties increased with the number of people to be accommodated, so that when the German Army marched into Prague on 15 March there were hundreds of German, Austrian and Sudeten nationals ready to leave with visas in their passports, for whom there had been no transport facilities. They had been accommodated in large camps, which became the Gestapo's first objectives. When they heard the news that the German Army was advancing, the refugees broke out of the camps and flocked to the foreign embassies in the quite vain hope of being given sanctuary. They had no money to pay for rooms, food or fares, but the Czech people, even in their own hour of crisis, did not fail them. They knew who were their friends and who their foes. They sheltered the refugees, they fed them and they hid them.

The Prague headquarters of the refugee organisations were raided immediately by the Gestapo.

The Czechoslovak Jewish refugees, who had less to fear from the Gestapo in Germany itself, where their names were not amongst the 'wanted' and whose emigration was, in one sense at least, desired, travelled by train from Czechoslovakia towards the Dutch frontier to reach England. Those who managed to reach Holland with papers showing their right to enter the United Kingdom before 1 April 1939 – the date on which visas had to be obtained by holders of Czechoslovak passports – were able to pass through, and in the tense fortnight which elapsed between Hitler's *Einmarsch* into Prague on 15 March and the deadline date for visas, the British authorities relaxed certain regulations and granted immigration to those refugees from Czechoslovakia who succeeded in reaching British sea or air ports, even if they could not produce evidence of future plans. This did not prevent parties of Czechoslovak arrivals (who had chartered their own planes) being refused leave to land at Croydon, and there were cases of such refugees being forced to return, while the detention of others in unspeakable conditions pending an investigation of their credentials and sponsors caused a minor scandal. The authorities had ostensibly made their concessions in view of the critical situation and the limited period before visas were required, which would automatically limit the numbers able to come. Pressure was brought by the authorities on the British Committee for Refugees from Czechoslovakia, formed primarily for the rescue of political refugees, to accept large numbers of racial refugees who were not necessarily those in greatest danger. The emergency was such that the demand could not be refused.

The plight of those who reached Bentheim on the German side of the Dutch frontier and were refused further passage by the Dutch frontier guards can be imagined. They had in many cases set out with no plans, or half-formed plans, for their maintenance in the United Kingdom. In the haste and confusion of their departure they had lost touch with the English refugee organisation with whom they had been negotiating such plans before 15 March and no one in England knew their whereabouts. They had left with little or no money, counting only on reaching Britain before 1 April. Now they had to spend the little money they had on telegrams and air-mail letters and wait for answers while the precious days ran out.

They hovered between Oldenzaal, on the Dutch side and Bentheim, on the German, in a frenzy of anxiety.

In England, guarantors had to be conjured out of the air, and still the desperate refugees arrived at Oldenzaal, penniless and in full flight, to be returned to Bentheim, or told by the Nazi authorities there that they must go to Cologne or Rheine and wait, as Bentheim could not contain them.

Only a fraction of those who reached the Dutch frontier were passed through before the visa regulation came into force, every case representing a separate series of crises in the offices of the refugee organisations in England, which made this the most critical 14 days in the whole history of the voluntary organisation system and came near to breaking it. When the strain was relaxed, it was found that hundreds of now completely destitute, homeless, planless and, of course, visa-less Sudeten, Czech and Slovak Jews were still massed on the Dutch frontier and were in imminent danger of being sent to concentration camps.

Those political refugees in Czechoslovakia who were not flushed out by Himmler and his infamous retinue of police spies and *provocateurs* within the first few days after the occupation of Prague tried to cross the Polish frontier illegally. The Polish frontier was very far away and they had no money. Some broke down half way. If they were not alone their fellows dragged them on. Many others were arrested by the Nazis as they reached the frontier. Some were shot at by frontier guards and arrived wounded on Polish soil only to be turned back by the Polish gendarmes.

At the end of March 1939, the British Committee for Refugees from Czechoslovakia sent representatives to various places in Poland to set up reception and clearing stations. After long negotiations the Polish government agreed to admit refugees provided they could go to other countries quickly. The old question of visas and transport arose again. The stream of refugees from Germany, Austria and the Sudeten areas had now been swollen by the Czechs, the Slovaks, the Hungarians from the areas ceded to Hungary, and the Carpatho-Ruthenians, both Jews and politicals. There was no outlet for the Polish anti-fascists from the areas ceded to Poland: they had the choice between a German prison and a Polish prison.

Most of the ships from Poland to western ports went through the Kaiser Wilhelm Canal. The political refugees could not risk travelling by that route. Special arrangements had to be made, again at great expense, to divert the ships round the Skagerak. Special ships were chartered to take refugees first to Sweden, whence they came to England. The delays grew worse – and were fatal. When the German army invaded Poland in September 1939 a small band of those who had escaped Hitler in Germany, Austria, the Sudeten areas, who had survived the invasion of Czechoslovakia, who had reached Poland after hazardous journeys, exhausted, starved and wounded, were finally trapped. There were some 1,600 refugees from Czechoslovakia in Poland; about 500 of these had already – either in Prague before the *Einmarsch* or in Poland – been accepted for immigration into the United Kingdom, but had been defeated by the delays.

They set out, marching eastwards, trying once more to escape their fate. They spent their nights in woods, their days trudging along on empty stomachs and bare feet. Over their heads the Nazi bombers roared. How they fared when they ran into the violent anti-Jewish pogroms in the Polish towns – that final degradation of a disunited people – one can only surmise.

About 50 refugees reached Rumania, and 100 got to Lithuania; many escaped to the Soviet Union; about 300 had fallen on the way.

Those few who were lucky enough to reach England from Poland before the outbreak of war arrived with nothing but the rags they stood up in, which they had been wearing day and night for months. Their physical condition was appalling and many did not recover.

The way of the political refugee, then, was unmitigatedly hard from start to finish. Wandering in circles, lost at night near an unknown frontier with certain death on one side and an uncertain future on the other, these men and women must often have faltered and questioned the purpose of going on. They had not set out on their perilous journey until their work was no longer possible and their lives were in jeopardy.

The forlorn hope of life and freedom, which could be shattered by a step or a voice in the hostile darkness, by a wrong turning, by hunger or exhaustion too great to be denied, could not have triumphed over despair in a single case had these men and women striven for their personal survival alone.

3

Immigration

The rescue and relief work undertaken by the refugee aid committees was strictly within the framework of the Aliens Order 1920 with its later amendments and such regulations as the authorities saw fit to introduce to govern its administration.

The Aliens Order is remarkable insofar as, unlike the 1905 Act (now repealed), it is itself merely an Order under the 1919 Aliens Restriction Act which entered permanently the emergency measures passed at the outbreak of the 1914 war into British law. By this 1919 statute, the Secretary of State was granted unlimited powers in regard to the admission and expulsion of aliens. This measure was originally designed to meet 'war, national danger and emergency'. The effective provisions of the Act have been renewed from year to year by the Expiring Laws Continuance Acts, which gain for it neither examination nor criticism, but the illusory cover of parliamentary approval. The Act, of course, does not take into account the special circumstances, nor recognise the existence of refugee aliens, and the granting of the right of entry is in point of fact vested absolutely in the discretion of an immigration official whose duty it is to keep out destitute or 'undesirable' foreigners.

The whole tenor of the Act, as one would expect from the circumstances and occasion of its original drafting, is rigidly restrictive. The rights of residence, settlement and employment as defined in the Act and the Orders in Council made under it are not, it is true, related to wartime conditions, but neither are they relevant to peacetime conditions, which create a million refugees. In particular, they assume a free right of return to the country of origin. In the matter of deportation the 1920 Order denies all justice and reason in a subtle subparagraph (subsection 'c' of Section 12) which gives the most far-reaching powers to the executive. The alien, in fact, has no protection whatsoever against arbitrary deportation at a moment's notice upon information supplied to the government in any manner and from any source, and there is no right of appeal or review. There is nothing to compel the authorities to grant the alien a hearing and the provisions of this clause are a blot upon the laws of this country, as their implementation in 1940 is a shameful episode in our history.

The Geneva Convention, ratified with severe limitations by Great Britain on 26 September 1938, was framed to meet the refugee problem. It laid down (in Article 9) that the application of laws and regulations for the protection of the national labour market should not be applied in all their severity to refugees domiciled or regularly resident in the country concerned, and (in Article 2) that such residence and sojourn should be granted to refugees in accordance with the laws and internal regulations of the country.

Unfortunately our Aliens Act does not permit of any but temporary residence, save in very exceptional circumstances – and in the Article of Ratification of the Geneva Convention, Great Britain specifically declared that Article 9 would not be applicable to refugees who had been admitted to the United Kingdom for a temporary visit or purpose (as most of them had in order to be admitted at all).

Similarly, Article 14 of the Convention provided that refugees should enjoy in the schools, courses, faculties and universities of the reception countries treatment as favourable as other foreigners in general. In particular, they should benefit to the same extent by the total or partial remission of fees and charges and the award of scholarships. Great Britain, in the Article of Ratification, declared itself unable to accept this.

In one further matter of principle, to which no formal exception was taken in the Ratification, Great Britain has failed to carry out the provisions of the Convention. It has denied the enjoyment of rights accorded to foreigners subject to reciprocity which were 'not [to] be refused to refugees in the absence of reciprocity' (Article 17).

As regards the clauses of the Convention under 'Administrative

Measures' relating to deportation (Article 5), Great Britain has taken care to safeguard the ugly provisions of the little subparagraph of our Aliens Order mentioned above. The protection which this Article sought to give to refugees was nullified by Great Britain's amendment that it would not be applicable to those who had been admitted to the United Kingdom for a temporary visit or purpose.

In brief, then, we have an illiberal and, in some particulars, even barbarous Aliens Act and a generous Convention relating to refugees whose major provisions have been modified, nullified or ignored by the British authorities who, ratifying it a few days before the Munich Agreement, declared it 'applicable only to refugees coming from Germany as defined, who at the date of ratification no longer enjoy the protection of the German Government'.

It was certainly not Britain's fault that, six weeks later, the most ferocious pogroms were organised by the Nazis; but who will doubt that the inertia of democratic governments and the inhumanity of immigration laws indirectly aided the persecution?

The Evian Conference of July 1938[12] was supposed to devise a workable international procedure for dealing with the refugee problem. The two salient features of this effort were, first, that 32 countries condoned by implication the organised robbery of émigrés by the German government and, second, that the Inter-Governmental Committee conceived by the Conference was still-born.

The effect of these circumstances was to develop, by 1939, a wrangling and haggling apparatus wherein the harassed but humane officials of both the refugee organisations and the Aliens Department co-operated to fit the refugee problem into the Procrustes' bed of the regulations. These ruled that permission to enter the United Kingdom would be granted to the following categories of applicants:

(1) transit emigrants – those with definite plans for further emigration within two years;
(2) children below the age of 18 to be prepared for emigration;
(3) persons between the ages of 16 and 35 for training with a view to later emigration;
(4) persons over the age of 60 (in the case of married couples the man's age alone being material).

Permission was subject to the conditions that:

(1) applicants did not undertake any work while in this country;
(2) a British subject acceptable to a refugee organisation or that organisation itself gave a guarantee of full maintenance during the period of residence in the United Kingdom and, in all cases except for elderly couples, bore the costs of emigration.

Our legislators argued that it was quite impossible to waive the guarantee-of-support clause without producing a storm of indignation amongst tax payers supporting, in January 1939, 1,918,583 unemployed nationals. Further, the regulation of 1939, requiring a refugee to produce evidence that his future settlement overseas would be effected within a period of two years as a condition of entry to the United Kingdom, remained inexorable, though the American 'quota' numbers ran into vast figures and the doors of the Colonies and Dominions were barred.

The 'exceptional cases' were as diverse as they were many. Every liberal-minded person must rejoice at the doggedness and ingenuity of the officials in the refugee aid organisations who fought for and found narrow but negotiable ways through the iron regulations.

Since no provisions existed to meet the case of refugees *per se*, in cases where they could produce no private guarantor nor any business proposition entitling them to settlement in the United Kingdom, nor any valid plans for re-emigration, they resorted to statements that they were students or visitors. They were consequently expected to return to their country of origin within a definitely limited period. To back up their assertions they were obliged to show that they had adequate means, and while some could borrow money for this purpose and send it back once they had been metamorphosed into refugees and accepted by a refugee committee after examination of their credentials, many more, of whom we shall never hear, were effectively prevented from coming at all.

The confusion, which arose subsequently because, in the absence of sane and humane provisions, refugees had been driven to obtain their entry under false pretences and their right to remain here was based on of plausible misrepresentations regarding their future, kept a small army of civil servants in a turmoil of unnecessary work for years. Meanwhile, and for the same reasons, the refugee organisations were prevented from embarking on the constructive task of rehabilitating the broken lives that they had saved. The disproportionate amount of work represented by the relatively small number of genuine refugees who came here under their own steam was due to the fact that, while they could not be repudiated by the appropriate refugee organisations, neither could they be accepted unless and until their tangled circumstances had been unravelled and their *bona fides* had been established.

The more far-reaching effect of the regulations, however, and the one for which they were presumably designed, was to keep working-class foreigners out of the country.

Let the British reader again think of the situation in the terms of his own countrymen. Suppose, let us say, that every Welshman was under pressure to leave the United Kingdom on pain of torture and death. For every well-placed Welshman of the educated classes, having good social connections and a familiarity with foreign countries, for whom the filling-in of forms and the completion of formalities, even under a hostile government, would be a comparatively simple undertaking, there would be a hundred others without the first idea of how to proceed. Someone would show him the ropes. Very well. But the London milkman, the Liverpool dock-worker, the miner from the valleys: whom does he know abroad by name, let alone well enough to approach with any hope of obtaining a promise of unlimited hospitality and support? Nevertheless, let us suppose that his situation becomes known and such a person is found, through his Union, or Welsh sympathisers on the continent. How does he then set about equipping himself with plans for re-emigrating to the far places of the earth (which demand considerable sums in landing-money), if it is laid down that he must leave home without even his paltry savings and must not earn his living abroad while planning to move on? The answer is that a camel could pass through the eye of a needle with greater ease and that your Welshman would stay where he was, as thousands of working-class Jews and endangered political anti-Nazis stayed in Germany and were bloodily murdered there.

At the other end of the scale were those freedom-loving Germans who, not themselves persecuted or interfered with, except insofar as their general interests were proscribed by a bigoted and harsh authority, preferred to leave the country either in protest at the treatment meted out to others or in prospect of a similar fate. They put their affairs in order, both at home and in the country to which they chose to emigrate, and set out. They were not 'refugees' at all in the technical sense, although their political sympathies might be wholly anti-Nazi, and as German citizens they enjoyed all the facilities of travellers in ordinary circumstances. For those bankers, industrialists and businessmen whose capital was internationally invested, the actual change of domicile represented a minimum of inconvenience and, though they were few in number and not generally referred to as refugees, the notoriety of one or two of them[13] has given rise to a certain anti-refugee feeling which their untypical position does not justify.

Facilities existed, in effect, in inverse proportion to the need to leave Germany and enter England.

Any attempted or actual contravention of the regulations on the part of the refugee committee meant forfeiting the goodwill of government departments, without which the work of rescue, as applied to thousands rather than individual cases, was impossible. The various aid committees depended upon the scrupulous observance of the rules and the correctness of their conduct for their existence.

It is a fact that without these committees exercising any deliberate discrimination or selection on a class-basis, the well-to-do, the well-connected and the non-political (racial and economic) refugee was in far the best position to conform to the regulations.

Employment

The same selective principle was at work when it came to the rights of employment and re-settlement. A businessman with even a little capital invested abroad to enable him to set up a commercial enterprise creating employment for British labour was, from anybody's point of view, a more welcome guest than the destitute working man. Apart from the 'individual producer' amongst professional people – the writer or artist, who could always do his work so long as the actual materials of his craft were provided by friends (although he could not always sell it) – members of the liberal professions were not allowed to work unless it was established that they had the blessing of the organised professional bodies in their own field and that the employment had either been specially created on humanitarian grounds and would not therefore displace a British subject, or that it conferred benefits upon the nation which were otherwise unobtainable. In practice this meant that, provided there was no professional jealousy – a factor that was not negligible – the lawyer, doctor, scientist, architect, teacher and so on, who possessed a highly specialised knowledge or technique, who could claim the patronage of unusually well-placed and well-intentioned colleagues, whose case could be put before senior people in the profession under the most favourable auspices and who could be shown to offer an outstanding contribution in his own sphere without creating competition, was permitted by the Home Office to work. The others were not.

The one exception to this was in the case of the medical profession to which, and despite considerable opposition, the British Medical Association, in conjunction with the Royal Colleges and the Home Office, admitted 50 Austrian and, later, 50 Czechoslovak refugee doctors to qualify for the British register and to settle and practise in the United Kingdom. The selection committee, composed of the most distinguished representatives of the profession, used as its terms of reference a scrupulous gradation of human needs in relation to medical qualifications, and ignored altogether the claims of money, influence or any extraneous circumstance. The man or woman concerned had to be, first, a highly qualified and experienced doctor with a family to support and, second, a genuine refugee with no alternative prospects here or abroad. This gesture was the more praiseworthy since it was made at a time when every conceivable restriction had been put upon refugees undertaking work in their own field and when the regulations that had previously admitted some 200 German doctors to the British register (provided they had the means to re-qualify and establish themselves) had been entirely superseded.

The medical profession also provides an interesting example of what is termed the 'benefits conferred' principle and its results. The insulin treatment of schizophrenia was far more highly developed and widely practised on the continent than in Britain a few years ago. Young German and Austrian specialists who were exponents of the technique were invited by hospitals and entitled by the Home Office to engage in its practice. Within a short time the refugee would naturally impart his knowledge to the British staff, whereupon he became not merely a supernumerary in the hospital, but an alien usurper and rival. His services were dispensed with and, having no British degree and no right to obtain one, he was thenceforth a useless burden on his friends or the refugee committees. The wide category of middle-class, middle-aged middlemen amongst refugees – extending from well-to-do merchants to small shop keepers – had no possibilities of work open to them at all, unless their friends could 'employ' them as agents – more often hawkers – for their own products.

Sir John Hope Simpson, in his classic *Survey* on refugees, put the figure of British employment as a result of refugee immigration in Britain at 20,000 in the summer of 1938. Sir Norman Angell has listed trades which by 1939 had been established in the special areas of Wales and the North-East by refugees and the numbers of British working people thus given employment. In this small book, *You and the Refugee*, the case for the refugees as an economic asset to Great Britain is pleaded so eloquently by Sir Norman Angell and Mrs Dorothy Buxton that nothing short of reiterating the arguments advanced there would serve the purpose of this present work. The value to a country with a declining population of absorbing men and women into its national economy, the expenses of whose non-productive period and training has been borne by other countries, is the main thesis of the case presented by Sir Norman, a case supported by every authoritative writer on the subject of population problems and the employment of immigrants and by an overwhelming mass of incontestable and objective facts. It is therefore only necessary to note here that these writers, these facts and this plea were entirely disregarded throughout the refugee era of 1933 to 1939 in Britain.

The fallacy in regarding immigrants as competitors in the labour market, as though work were a static lump to be parcelled out and were not created by the additional numbers who absorb consumer goods, is likewise exposed in *You and the Refugee* and, similarly, the facts were neither disputed nor refuted but merely ignored.

Re-emigration

In questions of re-emigration, the balance was strongly weighted in favour of the rich and cultivated refugees – the businessman with connections all over the world, the widely travelled or internationally known artist, scientist or other professional man – and was equally weighted against those whose chances of settlement and employment in this country were lowest, or nil. Nor was this disequilibrium corrected in the case of those who had genuine cultural and scientific benefits to offer and who were prepared to take their chance in the most remote and backward parts of the globe. This pioneer spirit coupled and imbued with European culture and science offered an opportunity for progress which could surely not be rejected. Rejected, nevertheless, it was: there were no 'openings' in the world for anything of that sort. Thus there was – to cite but one example – the 'Bata Unit', a group of young doctors from the great hospital run in conjunction with the Bata shoe factory at Zlin in Czechoslovakia. Composed of physicians, specialists and nurses, equipped for a complete medical service, including radiological and blood-transfusion apparatus, the unit was ready to go anywhere and to start from scratch. While in certain parts of the British Empire there is one doctor to every 100,000 persons, it was not found possible to 'place' the Bata Unit.

As the stream of refugees became a river and the river a flood, it was plain that nothing short of joint government action of the countries, Colonies and Dominions concerned to organise mass resettlement would address the problem. The amount of time, money and energy expended on individual re-emigration was out of all proportion to the results achieved, while, as in overcoming the hindrances to immigration, officials' time was taken up at the expense of the more fruitful work of planning the future absorption of refugees on a scale commensurate with the problem.

Whereas the possession of a number on the United States 'quota' and an affidavit certifying support – the two essential prerequisites for re-emigration to America (and not, of course, obtainable by those who dared not venture near the Gestapo-watched Consulates and had no wealthy friends in the United States) – had at one time satisfied the British immigration authorities, the regulations of 1939 required that before admission to the United Kingdom could be granted the 'quota' number must be low enough to denote a reasonable chance of being reached within two years, a condition which became increasingly difficult and finally impossible to fulfil. Hundreds of refugees who had American affidavits, but were assured by anyone in a position to know that their visa on the 'quota' would not be issued within three or four years, were terrified of advancing this as grounds for an application to obtain a labour-permit. They preferred to lie low rather than admit the truth about their hazy 'future plans', in case their very right to remain in Britain at all was challenged and their extension of permit refused. They did, however, join the overcrowded ranks of their fellows in a sterile, heartbreaking search for some alternative and earlier outlet overseas, thus increasing the competition for the few coveted openings which occurred. Since they were eventually to emigrate to the United States, nothing would have been simpler than to devise a policy to meet the case of these long-term transmigrants: a policy which permitted them so to occupy their time that, during the waiting period, they became morally and occupationally fitted for resettlement. The lack of such a policy had positively bad effects on the refugees as individuals.

It has been said by experienced workers in this field that the moment of arrival in this country was the only happy one the refugees ever knew. That may be an exaggeration, but there can be no doubt that a gradual and grievous deterioration set in for many of them when, after the first overwhelming relief at being safely out of a Nazi country had worn off, they were harried and frustrated at every step. Forbidden to work, to become self-supporting; perpetually battering at some hare-brained plan for re-emigration or pursuing the chimera of the purely fantastic schemes evolved from time to time by governments, it is small wonder that their vitality declined; that, from being creatures of revived hope, resolved to meet every hardship in rebuilding their lives, they became dispirited loafers, or importunate cadgers, besieging the refugee organisations day in and day out, banging other people's desks and shouting or, with distressing humility, begging for little special favours. It is small wonder that they resorted to backstairs manoeuvrings, to 'influence' – if the poor devils had any – to pathetic string-pulling and to more antipathetic practices in order to find their way out of the trap of compulsory idleness and vain scheming for a future.

In this respect the political refugees stood out in marked contrast to the racial victims. No doubt because of the conscious part they had played before emigration and the hope of a future that they would consciously seek to shape, the more tragic signs of discouragement and demoralisation seldom manifested themselves amongst the anti-fascist political refugees.

This superficial glance at the conditions of immigration, sojourn and resettlement of refugees in Britain barely touches on the appalling general waste of skill and labour, on the throwing away of the assets of character and intellect and talent which such treatment erodes; it makes no more than casual reference to the prodigious misapplication of administrative effort by staff in the refugee committees and minor officials in government departments; and it does not even attempt to describe the subjective effects of these conditions – the anxiety and disillusionment and despair – on the refugees themselves.

It does, however, suggest unequivocally that those conditions favoured the more privileged amongst the sufferers from Nazi oppression and disqualified, or put at a prohibitive disadvantage, the unprivileged. Not until post-Munich public opinion forced the government to admit refugees to Britain regardless of their economic status or personal connections was the balance of social composition slightly redressed.

NOTES

1. Simpson, Sir John Hope, *The Refugee Problem: Report of a Survey* (London: Royal Institute of International Affairs, 1939), p. 137.
2. Ibid., pp. 137–8.
3. We are concerned solely here with pre-war refugees. It is to be noted that the two German spies executed in Pentonville Prison in December 1940 and flamboyantly publicised as 'bogus refugees' arrived in this country after the outbreak of war and were detained.
4. House of Commons, 10 July 1940 (*Official Report* (*Hansard, Parliamentary Debates*), Vol. 362, cols. 1235–6).
5. House of Commons, 26 November 1940 (*Official Report*, Vol. 367, col. 81).
6. The Duke of Devonshire, replying to the Debate on Internment, House of Lords, 15 August 1940 (*Official Report*, Vol. 117, col. 263).
7. 'If you, Sir, were enlisting members of the Secret Service – which, of course, is in no way one of your functions – in order to obtain a clear insight of what was going on in Germany, would you send to that country people who talked but imperfectly the German language? Nearly all these aliens, although some of them have been here for about six years, speak such English that in many cases I cannot understand them. Nobody would ever mistake a refugee for anybody but an alien.' Colonel Wedgwood, House of Commons, 22 August 1940 (*Official Report*, Vol. 364, col. 1563).

8. *Lettre de Démission de James G. McDonald, Haut Commissaire pour les Réfugiés (Israélites et autres) provenant d'Allemagne, adressée au Secrétaire Général de la Société des Nations*, 27 December 1935 (Série de Publications de la Société des Nations, XII.B.2, 1936).
9. At the end of 1938, the number of political prisoners, as distinct from Jews, in concentration camps in Germany and Austria was approximately 400,000.
10. Sir John Hope Simpson's *Survey* shows that by the end of 1933 about 51,000 Jewish emigrants had left Germany, while the figure for non-Jewish refugees was 9,000. By December 1937 these figures had risen to 140,000 and 15,000 respectively. It must be borne in mind, however, that the figure of Jewish refugees includes a certain number of politicals of Jewish race. In Britain the disproportion of Jewish to political refugees was even greater, but was slightly redressed by the immigration of German and Austrian political refugees from Czechoslovakia between October 1938 and September 1939.
11. These were visas granted to categories of refugees rather than individuals and it was left to the leadership of the respective groups or political parties in Czechoslovakia to allocate the visas to those of their own members who were in the greatest danger.
12. The Conference was convened on the initiative of the United States government and was attended by representatives of the following states: the Argentine Republic, Australia, Belgium, Bolivia, Brazil, Canada, Chile, Colombia, Costa Rica, Cuba, Denmark, the Dominican Republic, Ecuador, France, Great Britain, Guatemala, Haiti, Honduras, Ireland, Mexico, the Netherlands, New Zealand, Nicaragua, Norway, Panama, Paraguay, Peru, Sweden, Switzerland, the United States, Uruguay and Venezuela.
13. For example, Mr Weininger and the Petschek family in the recent Boothby Enquiry (*Select Committee Report*, 18 December 1940).

The Refugees and the British Public

The right of asylum – Significance of the nationwide network of refugee relief committees – Public responsibility as a substitute for government action

1

The British reader may have interpreted the preceding section as a plea for the unlimited and unconditional admission of aliens to this country. Remembering our own two million unemployed of January 1939 – the peak of the refugee era – he may resent so partisan a view. But it is not the view implied here. Limited and conditioned the admission of aliens was bound to be; what was needed was an immigration law based upon the principle of the right of asylum and that this principle should be the sole guide in determining the limitations and conditions.

In practice this would have meant that, whether with or without means, with or without plans for re-emigration, with or without a personal acquaintance rich enough to support him, a man who could satisfy a competent authority that he was in fact persecuted in and driven from his own country by reason of his race, religion or politics would have been admitted here pending an examination of his credentials: a sort of Ellis Island. Once his *bona fides* were established in the course of a thorough investigation undertaken by persons with a genuine knowledge of the background of refugee emigration and in consultation with responsible refugee representatives, the immigrant would be allowed to take his normal chances of becoming self-supporting within the laws and customs of this country. If this appears unreasonable, what is one to make of the fact that some thousands of German nationals who were not refugees were living and working here before the war as businessmen, teachers, waiters, domestics, clerks and so on?

To bring about a state of affairs which enables the persecuted and oppressed to find sanctuary as free men a consistent pro-refugee policy is needed and not an anti-refugee policy with loopholes. Had evidence of anti-Nazi convictions and antecedents been the test for admission, there would have been no necessity to set up the elaborate machinery of tribunals after the declaration of war and, in the last resort, to turn upon the whole body of refugees and subject them to every brutish humiliation civil and military administration can devise. Had the government of Britain upheld the right of asylum for those whose life was in danger and whose need was proved, what Briton who loved freedom and hated tyranny would have protested if his fellow-worker, loving what he loved and hating what he hated, had spoken in another tongue?

The ambivalent attitude that did service as a refugee policy in all these years (and which gave the Nazi and the pro-Nazi facilities denied to the refugee) fed xenophobia. It is useless for government spokesmen to wail that the task of securing the safety of the British people against the machinations of these alien hordes was not an easy one. If danger existed from these quarters – and that it was grossly exaggerated is evident – then it was due to the lack of discrimination, or perhaps the wrong sort of discrimination, on the part of the authorities responsible for immigration.

2

The immediate effect of granting full asylum to the opponents of fascism – whether from Germany, Austria, Czechoslovakia, Italy or Spain – would have been to annoy the governments which had victimised them. That, of course, is some explanation of the attitude towards political refugees adopted by Great Britain, for to offend the fascist governments was not British policy in the years before September 1939. A further but even more immediate effect would have been to displease our own homegrown fascists and that strong body of influential politicians alive to the necessity of maintaining the social and economic structure of the fascist countries. To these people the extermination of the active opponents of fascism was an eminently sensible move and to admit them here from foreign countries, and thereby save them, was a criminally foolish one. Nor would the annoyance caused to the fascists at home and abroad have been mild or entirely simple. By the mere fact of granting such asylum the reception country tacitly condemns the excesses of fascist persecution, if not the system of which the excesses are a component part, and gives eloquent encouragement to those who remain opposed to the regime within fascist territory, whilst at the same time the anti-fascist forces in the reception country itself are stimulated and strengthened.

There is scarcely a single British citizen who has come into contact with refugees from these countries and who has not thereby become more conscious of the nature of fascism, learning to hate and fear it. This is true of contacts with all refugees. But when they are political refugees who have played an active part in the opposition, then far-reaching effects of a political nature may result. It is one thing to feel a generalised loathing for cruelty and tyranny and intolerance, but quite another to be made aware through a human personality, a living witness to the reality of the purpose and basis of fascism, of the other great forces surging under the currents of national life in fascist countries. To learn from a man's own mouth why he has suffered and fought and endured and refused to be subdued is to become, if not an adherent to his cause, at least an opponent of his enemies. The spread of such ideas was very much discouraged in high quarters and political refugees were consequently a minority. Even without the presence of political refugees, no policy of appeasement and non-intervention could meet with an entirely favourable reception from a public which, in almost every corner of the British Isles was liable not only to make contact with but to devote a good deal of cash and care to some family or group of refugees in the neighbourhood and to learn at first-hand, in the terms of human misery, what appeasement and non-intervention cost.

One has only to consider the response to the appeals by the Baldwin Fund,[1] the Lord Mayor's Fund,[2] the *News Chronicle* Fund[3] and the many privately organised large-scale charities for refugees[4] to realise how strongly the public as a whole felt about these claims upon its sympathies. If this public response may be taken, and it must be, as a substitute for official Britain's welcome to the refugees, then it may be conjectured that these millions of subscribers favoured some form of prevention rather than relief and viewed with alarm the load of suffering represented by every fresh, uncurbed, condoned accretion to fascist power.

In short, then, while the public indicated its approval of granting the right of asylum to the refugees from Nazi oppression in very material form, the government was able to hold a neat balance between home policy and foreign policy. It might, within strict limitations, admit fugitives to these shores at the expense of the charitable public; it need not thereby commit itself to any explicit aversion to the refugee-producing governments. Coping with refugees was a matter for private enterprise. At the same time the government gave the endeavour its formal blessing and thereby disarmed its critics at home.

In the belief that this attitude had changed at long last in September 1939, thousands of refugees flocked to offer their whole-hearted services to Britain. They were answered nine months later by internment, imprisonment, deportation and death by the mis-adventures of these three. The change was not of the nature they had supposed it to be.

3

Enough has been said to show that the refugees had considerably more reason to be grateful to the British people than to the British government. While the size of the contributions to the various refugee funds alone bear witness to the sympathy of the public for the refugees – as do also the constant championing of their cause by a number of forthright Members of Parliament and the steady devotion of hundreds of unpaid or underpaid workers in the refugee organisations – little has ever been said or written about the relief committees which were spontaneously formed, financed and voluntarily staffed by artists, architects, journalists, lawyers and youth organisations for their refugee opposite numbers. These were quite distinct from the nurses', doctors', agricultural, domestic, children's and trainees' committees which, with other specialised bodies, formed part of the central organisations. Nor has any tribute ever been paid to the countless voluntary committees formed in towns, villages and country districts throughout the United Kingdom.

The remarkable thing about the local committees is not that they sprang into being – everyone knows the English passion for serving on committees and the inexhaustible supply of ready-made committee men and women in every British hamlet – but that these bodies, for years on end and, in most cases, without official recognition, subsidy or so much as a say in the affairs of the central refugee organisations or their policy, carried the entire burden of looking after the refugees who had drifted or had been drafted into their neighbourhood.

Their function demanded the combined talents and skills of a mother, a hostess, an accountant, a labour manager, a language teacher, a psychologist, a solicitor, a Public Assistance administrator, an education officer, a trained nurse and a philosopher. It further required fluency in German, the patience of a saint and the tact of the devil himself.

It does not of course follow that every member of every committee embodied all these virtues. In practically all cases, however, the refugee under the care of a local committee received the most conscientious and personal attention and was more truly befriended than those of his fellow-exiles who remained under the necessarily more impersonal protection of the big central bodies.

These local committees owed their origin in many areas to the Spanish Civil War when the 4,000 Basque refugee children, after a preliminary stay in a camp, were dispersed to homes and hostels and institutions throughout the country. These young émigrés – the most helpless as they were amongst the most appealing of all contingents of refugees – needed local and immediate aid beyond that which could be provided by the parent relief body. English kindness and practical good sense came to the rescue in providing cash, clothes, furniture, lessons, advice on local conditions and the various other means of making the children's lives happier and more homely.

As in so many other matters, in this experience also the Spanish Civil War proved to be the 'try-out'. By the time the Austrian *Anschluß*, the cession of the Sudeten areas and the extradition of refugees from Czechoslovakia had created a refugee problem of proportions unknown in Britain, men and women were already mobilised in the localities who were experienced in working together and whose sympathies were wholly with the refugees.

Although it is generally known that the refugees, in the majority of cases, depended upon the funds and administration of the relief organisations as a whole, it is doubtful whether one can appreciate what it means to provide for the every need of some tens of thousands of destitute foreigners. It was not as though they were being gradually assimilated into national life. Had this been so, they would have needed only aids to independence. Nor did there exist – apart from those organised privately by the refugees themselves – centres for the social and cultural life of the exiles to make up for non-participation in British institutions. For these reasons it was not possible to look upon case work for refugees in terms of Public or Unemployment Assistance.

An Englishman and his family, maintained at subsistence level on unemployment benefit, subjected to a means test and living in conditions quite incompatible with scientifically established and universally acknowledged minimum standards of health, has still precisely what the stranger has not: relatives, neighbours and friends, a Trade Union, the 'reserve', if such it can be called, of furniture and household equipment, the right to draw upon the social services for himself and his family, and that invisible but priceless possession: the sense of 'belonging' to his home, his street, his district, town or village. This is not to suggest that the pinched and thwarted life of those enduring prolonged unemployment was gayer than that of the refugee. The argument is that while damage enough is done to your own people in these circumstances, you cannot even keep a refugee alive if you maintain him strictly at the level of, and in the same environment as, your own least fortunate citizens.

For example, let the pre-war Londoner go to the slums of Bethnal Green or Islington, or the Northerner to the back streets of Manchester and Hull. Then let him picture walking into those quarters a foreigner, not even speaking English, not even of the working class and wearing, since they represent the total wealth he was allowed to take with him, clothes which excite as much comment by their quality as by their unaccustomed cut. Does anyone think that the ordinary housewife in this street with a spare room to let, or the 'apartments' landlady or the boarding-house keeper will take in the foreigner for the same price as she would charge a recognisable and therefore acceptable member of her own class and nationality, or take him in at all? Suppose, however, that, in defiance of her own prejudices and misgivings, the advice of her neighbours and the whole tradition of the area, she was induced to do so, how would the foreigner fare at the local shops, without the language, handling an unfamiliar currency, having lifelong tastes – and perhaps as a result of health impaired by physical torture and privation, more than mere tastes – for foods other than those he can afford to buy? He does not go out to work like other men in the street; he cannot join their social life. This 'separateness' breeds further exclusion. He does not learn their customs or share their interests; he cannot assimilate their outlook or play his part in their day-to-day problems from which his idle and parasitic existence excludes him; their clubs and organisations are not for him. His status entitles him to no place in the life going on around him. He remains what he was: a stranger who can only buy that little margin of social 'acceptability' which lack of the right to work prevents him from gaining by his own efforts; and this is in no sense to criticise the hospitality, within their means, of every class in Britain. When it is a refugee family rather than a single individual, the case is harder: the needs are more diversified, the difficulties multiplied.

The moral, physical and intellectual decline to which the subsistence level of maintenance reduces all but the strongest characters cannot but take an anti-social turn in the case of these refugees who ask for nothing but to be allowed to start a new life in a new country. The political refugee regards his exile as temporary and the hope of returning to, and playing a part again in, his own country will carry him through hardships insupportable by the racial refugee, who has finished with his past and must take root in exile or have no future at all. In other countries, wherever refugee relief has broken down and the standard of living of this peculiarly extra-social section has fallen to that of the most indigent citizens, it has been observed that the refugee's morale drops not merely to zero but to a minus quantity.

By acquainting the refugees with the language and usages of this country, by arranging such matters as their medical treatment, their children's schooling, their supply of clothing, by indicating ways in which they might occupy their burdensome leisure and encouraging them to exercise their personal gifts and talents, by helping them to organise their own clubs and choirs, and by performing these functions with kindness and understanding the local committees stayed the process of disintegration.

Almost every refugee who reached this country left behind him relatives and friends – often in circumstances of grave danger – for whose rescue he felt pledged to work unceasingly. It was sometimes only in the belief that this was the one means of helping those others that individuals had resolved to emigrate. Once they had arrived in safety themselves, because they were offered private hospitality in or directed by the organisation responsible for them to the provinces with no access to the central authorities, they felt powerless to carry out their mission. Here again the local committees performed a service of immeasurable value: by conducting the official correspondence, and making the necessary applications they proved their concern for the refugees' interests.

Personal friendships and mutual appreciation between the committee members and their protégés sprang up to sweeten the labours of the one and the exile of the other. 'Difficult' refugees, trouble-makers and neurotics found themselves obliged to conform up to a point to the communal welfare watched over by the committees and, although intrigue is never far distant from refugee circles for reasons which will be discussed further on, its worst abuses were obviated as long as the committees remained alert and in the right hands.

Each local committee, although officially bound by the central organisation's instructions regarding the maintenance and care of refugees, had necessarily to exercise its own judgment and discretion in matters affecting the day-to-day lives of its own group. In this, as in the administration of funds – often collected locally – a vast amount of work was done voluntarily by social workers and accountants, both amateur and professional.

Why, it will be asked – and committee members must sometimes have asked themselves – this unstinting sacrifice of time and effort? What induced all these ordinary British people to assume gratuitously such heavy responsibilities when the authorities were probably doing all that was necessary? How had they come to regard themselves as the custodians of the British traditions of asylum which had been officially jettisoned? The questions are not purely rhetorical. The impulse to help the broken and wretched is not a rare or a national prerogative. The British character is sturdily developed in this, but that alone will not account for the nationwide network of refugee committees. Nor will it account for the even more intimate personal sacrifice represented by the thousands of offers of private hospitality to refugees. Before the war, the privacy of home life was most jealously guarded by the average Briton. Yet without the pressure of necessity, and sometimes in circumstances which meant great inconvenience to the householder, home after home was opened to the refugees. They were not always entertaining or even very gracious guests: they were often sick, nervous, querulous, unhappy individuals as a result of their experiences; they frequently took for granted gestures of the purest self-denial and, while many genuinely enriched their hosts' lives, it would be idle to pretend that, with their completely different habits – far more difficult to assimilate than those of urban evacuees in rural areas – their presence was always a success.

4

When Hitler came to power in January 1933, the average non-political Englishman gave this news item no more attention than he had accorded the other three changes in the German government during the eight previous months. But with the Reichstag fire – the greatest provocation since the burning of Rome by Nero – he was made aware of a new and very sinister influence on the continent.

The results of this conflagration aroused a fierce indignation in the minds and hearts of people who had previously shown no interest whatever in foreign politics and who now, and for the first time, realised the menace to life and liberty which the 'awakening of Germany' by Adolf Hitler represented. Upon this new awareness fell the successive shock of the Jewish pogroms, the burning of books, the revelations of the *Brown Book* and the Leipzig Trial. Hardly a single liberal-minded Englishman or woman was unmoved by the awful proximity of this violent return to barbarism.

The international protest movement received a very special impetus in Britain by the holding of the legal inquiry into the Burning of the Reichstag in September 1933, for which witnesses were brought to England by devious means to give evidence. With the complete breakdown of the case against the accused at Leipzig, with the acquittal and, finally, the release of Dimitroff, whose speeches in Court had echoed throughout the whole world, people everywhere became conscious that the spontaneous protest movement had actually contributed to the saving of those lives. These events were the precursors of and the stimuli to the anti-Hitler refugee movement in Britain. Meetings took place throughout the country and people who had never before been interested in or associated themselves with politics pledged themselves to aid the victims of fascism.

While the big Jewish organisations, which had set themselves the task of rescuing those who were being persecuted by Hitler on racial grounds, appealed to a rich community of co-religionists, a consistent campaign on behalf of the active anti-Hitler fighters drew coppers and silver from the pockets of the working class and from an ever-growing circle of English anti-fascists.

It was very soon realised, however, that the National Government did not share in the abhorrence of the Third Reich. The former fire-eaters and patriots of Whitehall and the City of London, who had sent a generation to die in 1914–18 that a tyranny less disgusting than Hitler's should disappear from the earth, and who had been hostile to the Weimar German Republic, were now bent on building a 'strong' Germany. The commercial travellers in diplomacy were busier than ever before. Organisations sprang up 'to promote goodwill and understanding' between Britain and Nazi Germany. Leading British statesmen constantly figured as guests of honour and speakers at functions arranged by these bodies, and contributed signed articles to pro-Nazi publications.

Events developed with terrifying swiftness – the Anglo-German Naval Treaty, the introduction of conscription in Germany, the occupation of the Rhineland, German intervention in Spain, the annexation of Austria, and the cession of the Sudeten areas – in all of which Britain, when not a partner, played a complacent role. Decent English people who saw these events against the background of unremitting and repulsive persecution of whole populations, became aware that help for Hitler's victims was not likely to come from the British authorities.

As the British government's appeasement policy reached its nadir in Munich, so the network of help for the victims of that policy expanded, although never quickly enough to meet the demand. With the cession of the Sudeten areas, the whole country was aroused.

Jews and democrats had suffered for years. From 1933 the horror of Nazi oppression, the torture of the Jews and the annihilation of political opponents had been known. Einstein and Haber, Bernhard Zondek and Heinrich Mann had been forced to flee; Hans Litten had been mutilated and killed; Edgar André and many others had been executed; Carl von Ossietzky, the Nobel Peace Prize winner, had been tortured and killed by the Nazis. But it was not until Munich that the persistent small-scale efforts and special appeals to aid the anti-fascists abroad crystallised into a drive in which responsibility was recognised and accepted by wide sections of the British people.

The crimes were not more horrible after the cession of the Sudeten territory than after the firing of the Reichstag; the brutalities were not more gross; the country immediately affected, as was pointed out to us, was one of which 'we knew very little', whereas Germany, the scene of the worst outrages on human life and liberties, was very well known.

What new factor, then, compelled British preoccupation with refugees and transformed that interest from a sectional one into a nationwide and vigorous movement?

Some felt guilt for the sufferings caused to a democratic people as the price of their own temporary security. Others, equally shamed by the diplomacy of Munich and the tidal wave of refugees that followed in its wake, felt that only by saving these people could we, and they, hope to see the troubled seas of international relations subside in peace. Others again saw in these refugees not the symbolic but the very material sinews of the anti-fascist fight. All, whether they discharged a personal debt or paid tribute as an oblation to the gods of peace, or felt solidarity with the trained and tried anti-fascists, were in fact demonstrating their sense of responsibility as a democratic people who respected the values being horse-traded by its government.

Hitherto the refugee committees, whether prominent, rich and Jewish, or obscure, poor and political, had found themselves hedged about and confronted at every turn by obstructive regulations.

Now that the matter had become one of national concern – no longer only to religious bodies, humanitarians and left-wing political parties, but a question embracing the larger one of the British people's principles – a marked change was apparent in the government attitude. The rescue of political refugees was accorded the stamp of respectability. It was openly mentioned in the Conservative press; new, subtle interpretations of the regulations were discovered by government officials, and refugee workers, almost dead from overwork, were revived by the stimulating effect of so much (temporary) benevolence emanating from the Aliens Department.

The rescue of political refugees was no longer a working-class affair, looked at askance by the authorities. Support for it had become too wide.

It is not only an irony, but a very illuminating comment on the contradictions of international politics and the force of public opinion that it was *political* refugees from Germany, Austria and Czechoslovakia who, in July 1939, became the main beneficiaries of almost £4,000,000 of British Treasury money.

NOTES

1. £485,725 from December 1938 to July 1939.
2. £360,000 within a few weeks.
3. £44,420.
4. Between the spring of 1938 and the autumn of 1939 British Jews contributed over £1¼ million to various appeals.

The Refugees in Exile

The principle of refugee representation – French and British pre-Munich attitudes to refugees compared – Types of refugees

1

The main relief organisations missed a very great opportunity in not setting up refugee advisory bodies to help in the management of the refugees' affairs. Perhaps because they were run on 'patriarchal' lines and although refugee helpers, sometimes working in key positions, were encouraged, they did not function so much as representatives of their fellows – although they obviously brought a special and valuable understanding to their work – but as loyal employees of English organisations. The important thing was that the large mass of the refugees had no voice and, what was equally important, no ear in the policies that moulded their lives in emigration.

On moral grounds alone, the sense of being required to participate would have been of enormous value to humiliated and demoralised spirits who suffered – the racial refugees more than others – from the cruel loss of self-respect entailed in being unable to support themselves and their families by their own exertions. On the practical side, the gain would have been immense, for however lavish the charity bestowed, it is bound to miss its mark if it does not take into account the actual requirements of its object and, since the charity of the relief committees could not be lavish, it would have been wise to consult the refugees on the most advantageous ways of dispensing what there was. To consult them, however, would have been possible only if broad sections – whether divided occupationally, politically, or in any other homogeneous grouping – had representatives who could have acted as an unofficial *liaison* between the mass of the refugees and the administrative bodies.

Only two such bodies came into existence in the refugee

movement in England, although countless minor examples of refugee representation and management of small communities – professional, cultural and residential – could be cited.

There were, of course, refugee organisations representing national or sectional interests, whose function it was to further the autonomous activities of refugees in spheres that did not touch their relations with the authorities, such as the *Notgemeinschaft Deutscher Wissenschaftler im Ausland*, the Free German League of Culture, the Council of Austrians in Great Britain, the German and the Austrian Self-Aid and the international Zionist OSE, whose headquarters were formally transferred from Paris to London shortly before the outbreak of war, and the various circles for refugee youth. While all these bodies were a great asset to the general welfare of the refugees, they were not primarily concerned to act as a bridge between refugee interests and the British administration of those interests. The one body which did attempt to do so, and failed, was the London Committee of German and Austrian Emigrants, known as the *Ausschuß*; the one that succeeded was the Working Committee of Refugees from Czechoslovakia, called the *Arbeitskreis*.

The advent in England, towards the end of 1938, of men and women who had played a prominent part in the affairs of pre-Nazi Germany, Austria and Czechoslovakia not only brought the *Arbeitskreis* into existence, but for a time gave fresh impetus to the older *Ausschuß*.

This latter body was composed of refugee personalities in the higher grades of their professions together with a few political figures. It was initiated by individuals who were mainly interested in refugees being assimilated into British life. They were not, however, elected by nor representatives of the mass of refugees, and for that reason alone (apart from the fact that they were seldom able to agree on any decision among themselves) they failed to act in the advisory and consultative capacity for which purpose they had come together.

The *Arbeitskreis*, on the other hand, consisted of representatives of the various national (German, Austrian, Sudeten-German and Czech), political and professional groupings who had fled from Czechoslovakia. It comprised 11 groups (three Sudeten, two German, two Austrian, one Czech and three groups which included members of all these nationalities in, respectively, racial, political and cultural categories). All of them, with the exception of the Czech group, had already existed in Czechoslovakia for the purpose of bringing their members to safety and had been recognised by the Czechoslovak Government Refugee Institute in Prague. The group leaders and their helpers therefore came to this country with a considerable experience both of refugee work and – what was in some ways more important – of the individual refugee and his history before his arrival here. Thus the Germans had helped to organise the escape and relief of their compatriots during six years in Czechoslovakia, and when the illegal crossing of the Polish frontier and the difficulties of political emigration finally had to be faced a highly developed system of mutual aid was already in being, so that the most endangered refugees could pass from friend to friend in their perilous flight. The refugees entrusted with this work abroad were persons of great reliability – indiscretion might have cost hundreds of lives – and they had to subordinate their purely political activities to the primary one of rescuing their political colleagues. This experience rendered the members of the *Arbeitskreis* indispensable during the critical and turbulent period of refugee work in Britain after the Munich Agreement. As soon as they arrived they set about providing detailed information concerning their fellows still in Czechoslovakia or Poland: their whereabouts, their credentials, their degree of peril, their personal circumstances, their suitability for further emigration and so forth. Without this refugee representation, many of the most valuable anti-Nazis would not have been saved at all. The group leaders set about mastering the intricacies of refugee administration in this country and put their time and energies and experience wholeheartedly at the service of the British Committee for Refugees from Czechoslovakia which had brought them to this country and was working for their friends. They continued throughout to represent their considerable membership – 50 per cent of all the refugees from Czechoslovakia – through the medium of this official organisation in an advisory capacity, although they had no direct dealings with the authorities.

It has been suggested that this refugee body was itself a political organisation and that it wielded administrative power. To its abiding credit, and in direct contradiction to this suggestion, the *Arbeitskreis*, despite its political composition, succeeded in gaining the almost unanimous agreement of its large membership to an official veto on participation in politics in this country. Similarly, far from exercising control, the *Arbeitskreis* performed the function of ensuring that official policy as laid down by the British administration was made known to, and faithfully observed by, the group members.

In considering the work of the *Arbeitskreis*, which was a completely new departure in the refugee movement in Britain, the reader will appreciate the value, to an understaffed and overworked relief committee, of exiles whose former position in their own countries had gained for them the trust and respect of their compatriots in emigration. For the refugees, and particularly the working-class ones who had only their native language and had never been abroad, it was as though the jungle had suddenly been signposted, and not for the refugees alone. While they could present their problems and difficulties to a group leader who, in the majority of cases not involving expenditure, could solve them on the spot, the relief organisation and its hard-pressed staff were spared the infinite repetition of the self-same information and could deal with one representative instead of a hundred or a thousand applicants requiring help and advice.

Membership of all save the Czech group and certain exceptional cases dealt with on their merits was confined to persons known and accepted by the groups in Czechoslovakia before their emigration to Britain. This meant that the group leaders, unlike the British refugee workers, really knew their people and did not have to waste time on establishing credentials and making preliminary enquiries before dealing with requests. There was therefore an automatic control on false claims or wrongful requests. The wiser members of the British staff came to rely upon the *Arbeitskreis* in the same way that its group members did and the strikingly high discipline on the part of refugees organised in this way, compared with that of unorganised refugees, fully justified the procedure.

With this excellent example of a refugee representative body and its saving of time, money and trouble to the relief organisations, one may wonder why the whole refugee movement did not adopt this system, and why it was left to the none-too-popular political refugees to do so. The answer is that while the Jewish and other organisations might have fostered an attitude of responsibility for their fellows, but did not, it had only emerged spontaneously among those sections who regarded their exile in social and not individual terms and who took the sense of solidarity which had characterised their work in the political field with them into emigration.

2

In order to get a better perspective on the situation in Britain it is worth comparing it with the treatment accorded to refugees during the same period by the other great democratic power in Western Europe, France.[1]

While Great Britain, during the years 1933–38, pursued a policy of highly selective immigration of refugees, the policy of the French Republic maintained the tradition of sanctuary for the persecuted. Certainly the attitude towards refugees fluctuated considerably in the course of these years – in accordance with the fluctuation in the internal political situation – deteriorating markedly with the fascist trend of 1934, and reaching its most favourable after the victory of the *Front Populaire* in 1936. It was not until the Munich period that an uninterrupted decline set in, ending in the complete abandonment of the policy of asylum and the internment of the anti-fascist refugees on the eve of the war.

During the years following the establishment of the Hitler regime there was a steady flow of refugees crossing illegally into France. Fugitives ran grave risks if they attempted to escape over the frontier. The German–French border country was not ideally suited for men and women who wished to escape the notice of the SA and SS; it did not, for example, afford the same protection as the Czech mountain ranges, but if a man's life is in danger he cannot select the easiest frontier – he has to take the nearest.

Were the refugees fortunate enough to dodge the Gestapo and reach French territory, with the help of a chain of well-wishers in the frontier districts who hid them during daylight, they could go to any gendarme and give themselves up as refugees. The French government recognised them as a special category of aliens. If their right of entry was questioned, they could appeal to special tribunals. It was rare for frontier officials to overstep their functions and drive refugees back to Germany. The important thing was that, however unconventional his arrival, the refugee had the right to claim sanctuary on the grounds that he was fleeing from religious or political persecution.

By a decree published on 23 September 1936, refugees from Germany who had arrived between 30 January 1933 and 5 August 1936 were issued with a *carte d'identité* (which incorporated the residence permit) as well as with a *certificat d'identité* (a travel paper), in return for which documents the refugee had to surrender his German passport. This condition was welcomed by the genuine refugees insofar as it drew a clear distinction between themselves and German nationals living in France; it allowed for no ambiguity and persons who did not wish to forgo the 'protection' of the German Reich, to which a valid German passport entitled them by law, or who wanted to go back to Germany occasionally to visit their families and friends, could not claim to be refugees.

Although refugees who arrived in France after 5 August 1936 did not come under the provisions of this decree, exceptions were made after that date in the case of political refugees or ex-prisoners from concentration camps.

The decision about whether someone's claim to be a refugee from persecution was justified or not was not left in the hands of ignorant officials. In 1936 a Consultative Committee was appointed by the French Government to examine all applications by Germans who wished to be recognised as refugees. The Consultative Committee was attached to the Ministry of the Interior and was composed of a French chairman, and four French and four German members, the latter being representatives of the four big refugee-producing categories: Jews, Democrats, Social Democrats and Communists. In general, the decision of the Ministry confirmed the recommendation of the Consultative Committee. The Committee was of particular value in dealing with the cases of refugees who, although they had been granted asylum on arrival, had been subsequently expelled, and had returned to France illegally. Their numbers had very naturally grown with the continuous increase in refugees coinciding with the reactionary period of French policy in 1934/35. It was common enough for people to be expelled from France and to go to Holland, or Belgium or Switzerland; to be expelled from there and to re-enter France illegally; to be expelled again and to cross into Holland or Belgium or Switzerland once more, only to return to France. From 1936, with the establishment of the

Consultative Committee, this position was regularised and genuine refugees were given full asylum and a recognised status until, in 1938, with the tightening of regulations and the desuetude of the consultative body, the number of refugees living illegally in France multiplied again.

The employment position of the refugees in France also underwent many changes in the period 1933–38, and it was not until the first Popular Front government that the refugee was given a distinct advantage over the ordinary alien in this respect. In 1932 it had been laid down that the Minister of Labour could allocate a certain percentage of foreign labour to each industry. This ruling applied to the millions of foreigners domiciled in France before the refugee-era of 1933. In most industries the proportion of foreign labour was fixed at ten per cent, although it varied in accordance with the distribution of French labour, as to both industries and areas. The German refugees in France from 1933 thus found ready-made ways for being absorbed into employment. Nevertheless they encountered great difficulties. Whereas Italian, Polish and Rumanian workers were common enough, French industry was not accustomed nor very well disposed to Germans. Moreover, the large number of professional workers amongst the 'new' refugees was not covered by the existing laws, although the labour market was never closed to them. With the anti-democratic moves in the 1934–35 period, labour permits were withdrawn from thousands of refugees, but with the improvements of 1936 it was relatively easy for recognised refugees to obtain a labour permit – if they could find a job. A considerable number of unemployables were licensed as small traders, or tried to earn a living as pedlars, but they mostly failed.

Whereas the position of refugees in France with regard to entry and the right to work was incomparably better during that period than in Britain, the actual relief work was very poor and the position of those who, by reason of age, health or previous occupation could not earn their living, and of those with heavy family responsibilities, was worse than in any other country where German refugees found asylum. But if there was little or no public responsibility taken for the refugees and no big charitable funds, socially and politically they received enormous support. There, more than in any other respect, the contrast with their position in England was most marked.

The two fundamental differences between the refugees' lives in

France and in Britain were (1) their right to organise themselves and (2) the very considerable political freedom that they enjoyed, which afforded them the possibility of continuing their own life as political elements engaged in the anti-fascist fight in some form.

They formed a strong and lively body to represent their interests both with the French authorities and in international relations. This organisation, the *Fédération Centrale des Emigrés Allemands*, did not have individual members but was a body to which organisations of refugees[2] were affiliated. It was recognised by the League of Nations and was represented by three members in the *Comité de Liaison* of the League of Nations High Commissioner. It was also recognised by the French authorities as the proper body with which to communicate on questions of policy relating to refugees from Germany. In this way the *Fédération* supplemented the work of the Consultative Committee of the Ministry of the Interior. Refugees from the other fascist countries had similar and separate organisations.

Although the refugees were not allowed to participate in French politics, they had great freedom to pursue their national political interests on French soil. They produced anti-Nazi papers and periodicals of every political shade for general circulation to German-speaking people all over the world, to which some of the finest writers and publicists in exile contributed and in which articles and reports smuggled out of Germany itself appeared. (Illegal editions of some of these papers were distributed in Germany under the nose of the Gestapo.) There were publishing houses run by émigrés solely for the purpose of producing German literature banned by the Third Reich. A magnificent library of the books burned in Germany was collected and established in Paris in 1934, and at a 'Free German University' lectures by eminent scholars were given to audiences of up to 200 students. The famous German Freedom Station, broadcasting every night, was assisted in its heroic work by anti-Nazis in France, who formed a delicate link between this ghost station and the outside world. The underground opposition parties had bases in France from which they could operate and thus assist and co-ordinate illegal work inside Germany. A People's Front Committee, under the chairmanship of Heinrich Mann, which sought to unite all the anti-Hitler parties and thresh out a common programme, functioned in Paris, from where propaganda material was issued and found its way into Germany.

All these activities, whose purpose was to assist the German people in their struggle against Hitler inside Germany, were supported by the whole body – the rank and file – of the political refugees and were not regarded as the special province of leaders and distinguished personalities. The latter formed a rallying point and directed the work but it was born of the dogged spirit of the mass of the political refugees, who felt a special responsibility upon them to work for their fellows in Germany still playing the hardest part.

A multiplicity of less directly political activities, all concerned with the welfare and support of the opposition inside Germany – aid for political prisoners and widespread propaganda on their behalf – were undertaken either by refugees or, at their initiative, by the French. In short, the political refugees in France were able to continue unabated in the service of that cause for which they had been exiled. Nor was French recognition of the legitimacy of these activities by political refugees on their soil merely tacit. Conferences and lectures, meetings and demonstrations, sometimes arranged under the auspices of refugee organisations and sometimes by French bodies, were jointly addressed by French and German speakers.

It will perhaps be thought that an idealised picture of refugee life in pre-Munich France has been presented here and set against one of sordid intrigue and demoralisation in Britain during the same period and that, if these pictures are true, then we must have been extraordinarily unlucky with the refugees who came here.

To correct this idea several points must be made and very clearly understood. Firstly, the political refugees in Britain did not undergo a wholesale process of demoralisation; the proportion of political refugees to racial refugees was very low in Britain and very high in France; and the *racial* refugees in France underwent precisely the same demoralisation or worse, for, while the right to work was not denied them, they mostly belonged to the wrong professions for large-scale absorption and had no private relief funds to draw on. Secondly, there were quite as many refugee political intrigues in France as in England, but the manoeuvres of the shady German reactionaries in France – whose opposite numbers in Britain gained credit in respectable and influential quarters throughout the period – were countenanced only in French fascist circles, which were themselves held in check by a strong popular movement in the pre-

Munich days so that these intrigues impinged hardly at all upon the lives and activities of the genuine anti-fascist refugees. A third fundamental difference was that these anti-fascist refugees were able to pursue their struggle against Hitler and had no need to canalise their energies and underground techniques into the stagnant backwaters of petty personal intrigue. For the political refugees in France, their illegal struggle had shifted from their own soil to that of a nation with a popular movement in the ascendant and a revolutionary tradition. Many former activities had to be abandoned but there were others to be initiated and developed and that shift, although it demoralised a few individuals – ill adjusted by temperament or by their experiences under the Gestapo – did not deprive them of their purpose in life. They were accordingly happier than in Britain, where a total discouragement of political activity, amounting to a ban, produced a state of suspended animation for those political refugees who were not personally engaged in welfare work for their fellow exiles and demanded of them a far higher degree of self-discipline that they might not lose all virtue in the standstill period of emigration.

Emigré politics everywhere and at all times have had the disadvantage of lacking a mass basis and inevitably give rise to 'personality' politics and parish-pump conflicts. This was true in France in the 1930s and the internecine warfare of the uprooted politicians was no less understandable there than elsewhere. The point is that in France and in all countries where the anti-fascist refugees were enabled to carry on their task of helping the living mass movement in Germany, there were real issues involved and the support and loyalty of the rank and file of the political emigration were at stake. This naturally gave a very different character to controversies there.

It was clearly shown in France that the political orientation of a government is reflected in its treatment of refugees, and fluctuations in French government policy and personnel were recorded very precisely in that treatment. At one point during the period refugee fortunes sank almost as low as in Britain but, for the most part, the refugees enjoyed a liberty of expression, a freedom of organisation and an acknowledged status never at any time accorded them in Britain. That fact makes the later and final deterioration of the refugees' position in France the more tragic. It was a true index of

France's own collapse. The fate of the refugees from the period of Munich until the time when the Gestapo combed through the refugee internment camps in France will be dealt with in a later section. Here it is only necessary to say that whereas Britain failed even to compete with France in its treatment of refugees when it was a liberal democracy, it took a feather out of its cap in imitating its later policy of ruthless suppression and internment.

3

Since the refugee relief movement was the work of private enterprise and was initiated at various periods by various bodies that had special interests in saving one or another of the persecuted elements – of which the Jewish organisations were the largest and the most important – there was no uniform or standardised treatment of refugees in Britain. At the beginning of 1939, when some 20,000 refugees from Germany, Austria and Czechoslovakia had reached Britain, when almost as many others were trying to gain admission[3] from Central Europe and the claims on the privately contributed funds were at their height, this lack of standardisation became highly detrimental. Fresh *ad hoc* committees, new co-ordination, and amalgamations of existing bodies and additional branches sprang up to meet the demand and in this reckless proliferation of central administrative organs, still largely in the hands of voluntary workers with an essentially humanitarian and not unemotional approach to the work, the refugee himself wandered in bewilderment from office to office trying to find his pigeonhole. With the growth of the organisations the refugee family unit was dealt with under different heads and even the needs of an individual – his housing, his employment, his future emigration, his children's education, his maintenance – concerned many departments, which were not particularly well co-ordinated. This decentralisation was quite inevitable and even justifiable, but in the hands of voluntary workers inundated with greater numbers of cases than any human being could possibly deal with, it was hardly surprising that the refugee who was a person and not a 'case' felt himself in a veritable jungle. Here more than anywhere else the essentially amateurish nature of the refugee aid work became plain. A great enterprise, involving the fortunes of tens of thousands of men, women and children, designed to meet the largest migration in modern European history, was left at the mercy of private benevolence and incompetence, both of which were at a singular disadvantage when brought up against fundamentally obstructive official policy. At the centre of the relief organisations there was specialisation without co-ordination (except in name); in the localities, where the close contact with the small numbers of refugees compensated for many defects, there could be no specialisation at all.

A definite line of demarcation was made and maintained between the refugees from Germany and Austria on the one hand and, on the other, those from Czechoslovakia (which included the Germans and Austrians who had fled to Czechoslovakia prior to its dismemberment). This distinction was laid down in a White Paper[4] of July 1939 when the Czech Refugee Trust Fund, a semi-government body, was formed to administer the unexpended balance of the British government's £4,000,000 gift to the Czechoslovak government, on behalf of these clearly defined categories of refugees. This brought the relief work for this section directly under Home Office and Treasury control, while all other refugees at that date were still supported by voluntary contributions and cared for by voluntary organisations.

Even here, however, the line wore very thin as it reached the provinces and outlying districts. The semi-government body owed as much to local committees as any other organisation. However often as its administrators might send out their *caveats* on this and that procedure, refugees in far-off Ayrshire and the Midlands still had their boots repaired and their aching teeth drawn according to need and the discretion of the local committee rather than by ordinance. If it was difficult to turn the voluntary organisation into the official organisation at the centre, it was impossible to do so in the localities – and undesirable. Many of the original local Jewish aid committees had taken on Czechs when they arrived in their district; some of the local Czech committees had become incorporated in the general aid committees in their area. To separate them again would have meant chaos and injured feelings, so the refugees from Czechoslovakia, with their preponderance of politicals, were dealt with by the same personnel who handled the German and Austrian racial refugees. This caused a certain amount of difficulty.

Refugee aid workers are distinguished by a very staunch partisan feeling for their 'own' refugees. They do not display hostility towards other types of refugee but, with pardonable irrationality, these are considered inferior and less deserving of the limited number of visas, or work opportunities, or opportunities to emigrate or to obtain free places at universities, or whatever else may be going. This competition on the part of the friends of the refugees had all the earmarks of a scramble for scarce resources and was no more than an eloquent comment on the official attitude, which allowed some refugees in if they could comply with inflexible and difficult conditions, which forced them to re-emigrate (but did nothing to open the Empire's doors), which refused to maintain them, but equally refused them the right to work and to maintain themselves.

As these circumstances bred competition amongst the refugee committees, so the competition bred a keener partisanship. People animated by the deepest benevolence in their work would shudder at the thought of helping an emigrant trade union official if so much as one distinguished refugee scholar was unrecognised. Others would not listen to the needs of middle-class Jews while the lives of political anti-Nazis were endangered. Some had ears only for the cries of agrarian youth destined for Palestine; others would have thought nothing of denouncing to the authorities any fellow-worker who stood in the way of obtaining privileges for refugee musicians as the agent of a foreign power. There were those who felt impatience with everyone who was not saving the children; and those who ploughed a lonely and a difficult furrow, arguing that the aged might have priority and end their days without violence. Some loved Austrians and thought ill of Czechs; others loved Czechs but despised Slovaks. All furthered the interests of their special category of refugees, pleading, persuading, string-pulling, cashing-in, turning to account and accepting no rebuffs, since this is what they were there for. No one could criticise these enthusiasts for their militant favouritism, nor detect in it that tendentiousness which later became a real problem and assumed a very sinister shape.

Active discrimination of this kind was not appreciable until, largely as a result of outside events, the differences between political refugees and every other category of refugees was recognised as fundamental.

The British Committee for Refugees from Czechoslovakia, a

voluntary organisation set up immediately after Munich to rescue the Sudeten refugees and others sheltering in Czechoslovakia, accepted, and succeeded in persuading to accept, the yardstick of 'those in the greatest danger' being allocated the coveted 'block visas' which meant, in effect, granting asylum to those who had been most active, most prominent and most uncompromising in their opposition to the Nazis. The economically displaced and culturally suppressed liberals had to give precedence to these marked men, who were being mercilessly hunted and done to death by the Gestapo, to the less immediately threatened racial victims, and to the more obscure though loyal anti-Nazis. Their friends in Britain were not pleased and vented their displeasure, not upon the government for limiting the visas so severely, but upon the committee which had set itself the task of saving those most liable to extinction.

The consequence was that, while a certain number of leaders and officials of the left-wing political parties, their colleagues from the illegal parties of Germany and Austria now unable to remain in Czechoslovakia, the most prominent trade unionists and outstanding anti-Nazi spokesmen and writers, and those who had played a public part in the Jewish organisations were brought to safety, a hundred thousand others with good reason to dread Hitler's rule remained behind. The 'discrimination' thus exercised by the Committee was reflected in a more hostile discrimination in this country against those so rescued at the expense, which no one denies, of an equal number of other different refugees who might have come in their stead.

This gave rise to one type of 'anti-political-refugee' motif and was played, in a very sustained manner, by the disappointed champions of the non-political victims in the new fascist areas. Theirs was a humanitarian and well-intentioned grievance. Whether their methods of campaigning were equally humanitarian and well intentioned, only they can say. One type of argument advanced by people with no lack of sympathy with refugees as a whole and followed in principle by the Jewish organisations was that the innocent victims had a first claim, since they had done nothing to provoke their own sufferings. The political refugee, on the other hand, whether Jewish or not, had deliberately engaged in activities whose consequences he must have foreseen and must have been prepared to face if he was worth his salt. By this argument no vile tyranny in history would ever have been overthrown, since opponents would have been exterminated and its innocent victims would not thereby have been lessened but, on the contrary, would have endlessly increased.

Another grievance against this well-defined group of refugees was based upon the fact that it included Communists. Communists had played a stubborn part in the anti-Nazi fight before Hitler's accession to power and unceasingly since that day.[5] This had been recognised all along by the Labour movement but, with the spread of the intense anti-Nazi feeling to all sections in this country precipitated by Munich, the fact became increasingly embarrassing to people who, although now anti-Nazi, were even more anti-communist. Nor were these Communist refugees, though small in number, admitted to this country under any other title. They were not argued away. Their political affiliations were recognised by the authorities; their grave endangerment and the understanding that they would not engage in propaganda or political activity in Britain were considered sufficient grounds for giving them asylum. Many people saw in this handful of hunted men and women the very shadow of Moscow lying over English homes and were not slow in saying so.

If the word 'Communist' evokes a violent reaction in some people, the words 'foreign Communist' more than double the effect; one has no need to magnify the menace conjured up by those two words in order to excite the deepest prejudice. When, moreover, these people are associated with that other prejudice-provoking word, 'Jew', there is no limit to the fear and hatred which artful propaganda may arouse, as has been amply testified in Germany itself. Since these reactions in their most naked form can only occur in persons addicted to emotion rather than reason, to feeling rather than fact, the actual numbers and the personal conduct of these Communist refugees could in no way modify those views or their expression.

The organisation which had the official function – laid upon it by the terms of the government White Paper – of caring for these amongst other political refugees, was itself accused of being a subversive body. Newspapers ran the ever-popular story of communist influence. By a neat transference, the administrators rather than the recipients of Treasury funds were accused of communism. These attacks both fed and were fed by, anti-Communist sentiment and laid upon the organisation the very special responsibility of maintaining a scrupulous impartiality towards the refugees in its care and not succumbing to the scurrilous campaign. This attitude was interpreted as positive proof that the organisation was subversive, and even some of its own local committees, observing that no action was taken to treat the Communists as a special outlawed category, got into huddles and produced excited memoranda to show that a very sinister influence must be at work in the continued maintenance of refugees to whom the government had granted asylum.

A third type of discrimination was due, as is so much of human error, to pure silliness – on both sides.

When the mists of romanticism or prejudice have been dispersed, the refugee emerges as a figure distinguishable from his fellow men by his lack of home and social roots, by his haunted memory, by his ever-present anxiety for those whom he loves and has left behind, and by that disorientation which is the product jointly of his exile and the factors that caused his exile. In other respects he is as other men: more-or-less gifted, courageous, honest, intelligent, loyal; foolish, vain, truculent, spiteful and shallow. Bereft, as he is, of the proper soil and the natural conditions for growth; torn out of his environment and with no outlet for his varying degrees of energy and initiative; reduced by the tutelage of an aid committee practically to the status of a child in all matters affecting the government of his personal and domestic life – and he has no other – it is small wonder that his worst traits are accentuated and his best stunted. It is hardly surprising that, in countless cases, the exact reverse happened: that in conducting themselves with dignity and discipline in these circumstances, and in giving leadership to their fellows, refugees have discovered a new self-respect and grown in stature. This is one of the most moving testimonies to the indestructibility of the human spirit and to the quality of the men and women whom Goebbels classed as subhuman.

Nevertheless, in idleness and unhappiness, considerable numbers of the refugees, erstwhile busy and important persons, found nothing better to do than to squabble and intrigue. Nor did these activities lack venom and it is quite certain that gentle English people, unversed in Central European methods and politics, drawn into refugee work by the wish to succour the helpless, were very much affrighted by this display of nastiness. Many refugee workers accordingly turned aside and resorted to very foolish and sweeping denunciations of all political refugees, desiring their removal from the community, not because of the high nuisance-value of certain individuals, which would have been quite sensible, but because they were all fiends in human guise. In their indignation the excited old women, male and female, who headed the Silly Brigade of discriminators forgot that those responsible for refugees cannot just 'clean them up' on the Nazi pattern when they fail to please.

It would be foolish to think that serious political intrigue was absent amongst refugees. That it should exist – though not in the quarters where it was most suspected – was inherent in the fact that every shade of political opinion was represented in the emigration from Central Europe. There were those who had held positions in the Nazi Party, or who had collaborated with it, and who had for some reason or other (often personal jealousy) fallen foul of the Hitlerites and left Germany. There were Hohenzollern princes and the faithful followers of 'Emperor' Otto von Hapsburg. There were the financiers who found the City of London a safer and more pleasant place than the Third Reich. There were the renegades from Left and Right, discredited conservatives and bankrupt Hindenburgians. By virtue of their social standing many of them moved in influential British circles where, although Hitler was not altogether liked, the idea of a left-wing alternative to him was positively abhorrent. In these circles a régime in Germany was favoured which, although just as reactionary and oppressive in internal politics (albeit a shade less sadistic), would not be so troublesome and aggressive in foreign policy. This is where the tame Nazis came in: they were regarded as a possible alternative to Hitler.

No genuine political refugee who had played a part in the organised anti-fascist movement in Germany (or Austria, or Czechoslovakia) claimed that the overthrow of Hitler could be effected by émigrés. But those other German 'leaders', with no following or basis in Germany, who professed to oppose Hitlerism feared nothing more than that the German people might one day take things into their own hands. They played themselves up as the 'future Germany' and did their best to discredit the democratic opposition movement and its adherents wherever they found them.

The political line of these discredited reactionaries was not the overthrow of the Nazi regime by the German people but a war against Germany at the end of which the Allied victors would put them back into their old positions. The extent to which they were accepted in influential quarters may be judged from the fact that, while most refugees were being put into gaols and internment camps, Prince Starhemberg, the Austrian fascist who was kept in office by Mussolini, received a commission in the Allied Air Force,[6] and almost the whole British press has represented the fascists Otto Strasser and Rauschning as distinguished representatives of the anti-Nazi emigration, whereas their histories make it perfectly clear that, but for personal differences, they would today be leading members of the Nazi government. It can also be seen in the composition of the new Czechoslovak 'government' set up with the blessing of the British government, and which includes two members of the 'Protectorate' Hacha government (set up by Hitler to do his bidding) and the late Inspector-General of Hitler's 'independent' Slovakia: elements as inimical to the Czechoslovak democrats in this country as in Czechoslovakia.

With the petty squabbles on the one side and the grand-scale manoeuvres on the other; with the existence of revolutionary elements amongst the refugees and the highly restricted and selected immigration of politically endangered persons, there was enough inflammable material lying about for mischievous persons to touch off. They lost no opportunity in doing so, and the outbreak of war was the opportunity *par excellence*.

NOTES

1. As the outstanding problem between 1933 and 1938 was that of the refugees from Germany and Austria, this section refers mainly to them, although, of course, the legal status was the same for refugees of other nationalities.
2. For example, the associations of refugee doctors, lawyers, writers, teachers, artists, women, youth organisations, and so forth.
3. Figures for immigration into the United Kingdom of Jewish refugees alone rose from 1,199 in the month of December 1938 to 3,895 in March 1939 and 4,333 in April 1939. In the previous year (1937) the figures had been 267 and 255 for March and April respectively.
4. Cmd. 6076, *Czech Refugee Trust Fund and Directions to the Trustees*, July 1939.
5. In July 1940 the Communist Party of Germany repudiated Hitler's Compiègne Armistice in the following terms:

> The terms of the Armistice signed in the forest of Compiègne on June 22nd do a monstrous violence to the French people …
> The subjugation and national enslavement of other peoples will never bring lasting peace but new and bloodier wars …
> The working people of Germany who bore the burdens and suffered the humiliation of Versailles, have no interest in nor the intention to allow the French people to be burdened by a new Versailles …
> The working masses of Germany … have nothing in common with these predatory elements in Germany …
> They [the German working class] are bound in solidarity with the cruelly oppressed peoples of Czechoslovakia, Poland and other countries occupied by the German army …

6. I want to know whether it is our money which is going to pay Prince von Starhemberg. We all know him. He is apparently now a French officer under General de Gaulle – a Jew baiter, a commander of the Heimwehr against the workers of Vienna. He ran away when the fight came, he ran away again when Dollfuss was murdered and again at the Anschluß. He appealed to Hitler to use his services after the Anschluß and was indignantly refused.

Colonel Wedgwood, House of Commons, 21 August 1940 (*Official Report*, Vol. 364, col. 1373).

The Doors Close

On the eve of war, there were approximately 65,000 refugees who had reached this country and who had not yet re-emigrated. For every one refugee in Britain there were many still abroad whose applications for immigration were pending, while the worsening conditions for Jews in the Czech 'Protectorate', in 'independent' Slovakia and in the ceded territories increased their number daily. There were Germans and Austrians still thronging the Consulates for their papers. There were Jewish and political refugees from Czechoslovakia assembled in Poland and ready to leave for England when, with the outbreak of war, the door to immigration was closed.[1]

The 65,000 refugees in Britain were composed of, roughly, 90 per cent racial refugees, of whom a certain proportion was also political in the sense that it consisted of those who had played an active part in Jewish public life and were for this reason, as distinct from the accident of their racial origin, in danger from the Gestapo. The remaining 10 per cent was made up of political refugees in the sense that, though they might or might not be Jews, they had taken an organised part in the purely political struggle against Hitler.

The majority of all refugees had no occupation. The exceptions were: holders of Ministry of Labour domestic permits; refugee couples employed in domestic service; nursing and midwife trainees (these being the occupations in which there was a recognised and general shortage of British labour); there were several hundred doctors practising or studying to re-qualify for the British register, as were also some 50 dentists; a variable number of young refugees was employed in seasonal agricultural work, while others were in some form of privately organised agricultural training. A few refugees with capital had established businesses, particularly in the distressed areas of Wales and the North-East; some were working as scientific, engineering or industrial technicians, while about 250 were continuing often unpaid research or academic work. To this must be added a far larger section of trainees in various trades and occupations; of men and women actively assisting in work for their fellow-refugees, either in the refugee organisations, or in clubs, hostels and residential institutions. Finally, there were 3,500 Jewish youths and men living in a refugee camp in Kent, where they were responsible for all services and were trained in the crafts required by the camp community.

Trainee permits as a means of entry to Britain were being sought with every other means of entry at a perpetually increasing rate, while applications for labour permits for refugees already in the country, with no immediate prospects of emigration, were piling up week by week in government departments. Many of those who now sought work had not practised their trades for over six years and had become what has been called 'professional refugees'; many more had been trained for callings in which no openings could possibly occur in any but their own country (such as lawyers) or from which the majority was excluded in this country (such as doctors). These categories, which embraced merchants and commercial or clerical assistants who desired retraining, represented the bulk of the refugees.

A standstill order on the granting of all working-permits was decreed as soon as war broke out. The door to employment was closed.

Owing to the temporary nature of their leave to stay in Britain, arrangements for the housing and general living conditions of the refugees were of a provisional character. The work of rescue had been the paramount concern of all the relief organisations; on arrival the refugees, for whom in any case little was done by way of rehabilitation, were housed in furnished rooms, in lodgings, or in hostels taken more for their capacity to accommodate large numbers at a low rent than for their suitability, either as regards situation or convenience, for permanent residence. The makeshift nature of the housing arrangements for all refugees not receiving private hospitality, and without the means to make their own arrangements, was due on the one hand to the relative unimportance of the problem compared with that of bringing the refugees out alive and, on the other, to the fact that permanent settlement and employment here were not on the official programme.

These refugees were in a physical condition that defies description. It was not merely that, through privation and torture, the refugees had contracted every variety of deficiency disease, but the conditions of their flight and exile – sometimes through two, or three, or four countries – prior to their arrival here, had induced in them a permanently lowered resistance which made them an easy prey to illness and an even readier one to imaginary ailments. The outstanding need for dental treatment alone bore witness to the poor state of general health – while the incidence of tuberculosis, diabetes, kidney disease and gastric trouble was higher amongst refugees than in any but the poorest sections of our own people; there were sufferers from psychological disorders varying from the chronic *malade imaginaire* – a very genuine condition amongst émigrés – to the nervous wreck bordering upon psychosis, with every conceivable variety of neurotic in between. No proper health services for refugees were organised, no survey was made, and these people depended for the most part on the generosity of individual practitioners who had offered their services to the refugee committees for their treatment.

At this period the vast majority of those maintained out of publicly raised funds was dependent upon charitable organisations. Only some 5,000 were supported by the special government fund granted to the refugees from Czechoslovakia. The charitable funds were no longer able to meet the growing needs of the refugees and, on 6 June 1939, the Chairman of the Co-ordinating Committee announced that the refugee funds were exhausted. By September, the weekly cost of maintenance represented some £14,000. At the outbreak of war, when the organisations had overspent their income by many thousands, no further appeals for this purpose could possibly be launched and many of the regular contributors were obliged to withdraw their support. Private guarantors who had undertaken an unlimited liability, but had counted upon the speedy re-emigration of their protégés, found themselves unable to continue maintaining individual refugees at a time when their own families were broken up by enlistment and evacuation. Thousands of householders dismissed their refugee domestics, either because of their changed circumstances or in sheer fright at having aliens in the house during wartime when the status of those aliens had not been defined by the authorities. All these refugees were thrown back upon the voluntary organisations, literally in thousands. Thus the finances of the refugee organisations which cared for the majority were at their lowest ebb and in the worst position to recover, while the charges upon them were greater, and increasing at a faster rate, than ever before, despite the end of immigration which had never at any time saddled them with such unforeseen commitments.

The local committees had depended upon subsidies from the centre, or upon private contributions raised locally, and were thus similarly placed: 'private' cases in the neighbourhood, of whose existence the committees had never heard, were suddenly thrown upon their care; while many of the most vigorous committee members were drawn off into some form of National Service, leaving weaker and less experienced bodies of people to cope with new and greater problems. The effect of the war situation on the privately organised professional aid committees was equally disruptive. Their leading personalities – themselves men and women of high standing in their own field – were absorbed into war work which removed them physically, if not in interest and sympathy, from the refugee work. All the smaller voluntary bodies shared with the large organisations the handicap of being unable to launch campaigns and public appeals on behalf of refugees at this time.

For the refugees themselves, the outstanding fact was the end of any hope of rescuing relatives and friends. The thousands who had enjoyed private hospitality or who had been in jobs and who were dismayed at finding themselves suddenly dependent on Committee maintenance; the enormous numbers who had accepted makeshift arrangements while they planned to go overseas – all were involved in the desperate last-minute rush to save those left beyond the frontiers. They came from everywhere, flocking to the central organisations, besieging the offices and rendering the work of dealing with the enormous new tasks that faced the refugee workers almost impossible.

At this point Warsaw was bombed; immigration of refugees into the United Kingdom ceased; applications for permission to remain or work here were temporarily suspended and emigration came to a virtual standstill.

The doors were closed.

NOTE

1. At a later date, and up to May 1940, individual immigrations of persons to whom visas had previously been granted by the British authorities, and who had reached neutral countries, were allowed. This permission was in respect of the wives and/or children (under 18 in the case of males) of refugees already in Britain.

Part Two

THE REFUGEE PROBLEM IN WARTIME

The Early Months

New regulations – The Army and employment –Tribunals – Worsening of conditions

1

At the outbreak of the 1914–18 war, almost all male enemy aliens in Great Britain, but not their wives, were interned. The services of these interned aliens were not used at first, but later, in a small way and eventually as a general practice, most of the able-bodied internees were employed in some capacity.

This war opened with about 75,000 enemy aliens in the United Kingdom, of whom about 65,000 were refugees, with a majority of Jews who were not recognised as German citizens by the German government. Those who thought about the refugees at all assumed at the outbreak of war that they were our friends, as surely as the Nazis of the Embassy and Consulate and the Hitler apologists of British nationality were our enemies.[1]

In refugee circles debate ran high as to what would happen to them: would they all be interned and then released on individual examination to reassure the British public of their *bona fides*, or would they all remain free except those against whom definite evidence of unreliability existed? Would they be expected to volunteer for the armed forces, or would they be encouraged to give their specialised services according to their abilities? Would they be examined by civil tribunals or by military tribunals, or would the organisations familiar with their cases classify them on the basis of their trustworthiness? Would they be regarded as friends or foes? Would they be permitted to remain here for the duration of the war, or be allowed to follow out such re-emigration plans as were in progress, or was it possible that they would be deported?

No refugee in his senses could possibly foresee that every one of these contradictory contingencies would come to pass and that, in the course of less than 12 months, he would be subjected to forms of treatment which, on the face of it, were mutually exclusive, but were nevertheless consistent in their most significant particulars. Had he foreseen this state of affairs he must have wondered, long before he found himself lying on straw in a rat-infested wharf behind barbed wire, or being shipped to Canada under military guard without his consent or the knowledge of his family, what the British thought they were fighting for if the first anti-Nazis in Europe presented such a menace.

As it was, however, in September 1939 the refugees presented themselves in their thousands to enrol for National Service, while others besieged the recruiting offices, government bodies and professional organisations to offer their services.

For the refugee relief organisations, equally in the dark as to the eventual status of their protégés in wartime, a completely new phase opened as, with heavy hearts, they relinquished the work of rescue which had brought them into existence. It became a matter of taking stock of those fixed numbers who were actually in Britain. There were, so far, no indications whether these refugees now here would be allowed to remain in England for the duration of the war, nor whether they would be able to work in industry or National Service if allowed to stay. Indeed, the fact that the authorities ruled it impossible to deal with new or pending applications for work permits caused even those who had jobs or training awaiting them to miss their chance. Employers had to make alternative arrangements as a result of this ruling while others, influenced by it, hastily dismissed their alien employees.

In this situation, while extension of leave to remain could not be applied for and emigration was suspended, the organisations were asked by the authorities to submit classified lists of the refugees registered with and known to their various departments and committees. They were to be listed under 'Known to be reliable', 'Insufficiently known' and 'Suspected of being unreliable'. It is true that these relief bodies, hitherto working under quite extraordinary pressure with the prime object of saving lives, did not have the qualifications of MI5, yet these preliminary classifications were based on a far wider knowledge and a far deeper understanding of refugee circumstances and politics, of the antecedents of the individuals and of their behaviour since immigration than any subsequent judgments and should have formed, in conjunction with Home Office and police *dossiers*, the basis for the formal sifting process that was later instituted. By the time they became relevant, these committee classifications appear, judging by results, to have been forgotten, lost or confused.

The responsible members of the relief committees supposed that the request for this 'stock-taking' indicated a sober and rational refugee policy in line with the Home Secretary's statements on this subject on the day after the declaration of war.[2]

The publication of the White Paper on the Treatment of German Nationals in Germany[3] confirmed this view. It seemed to the refugees and their British friends alike that after seven years of shameful silence and acquiescence in the face of the most monstrous organised cruelty the modern world has witnessed, the British government had taken a stand on the question of Hitler's victims. The horrors described, which had been fully realised by those in contact with the refugees, were at last made public. Here was an official publication which implicitly championed the persecuted and oppressed and thereby drew a distinction between Hitler and the German people.

This marked the only occasion on which the government issued a statement calculated to excite sympathy with the German victims of fascism. It is significant that this statement was withheld until after the outbreak of war,[4] when nothing further could be done to rescue the victims of the atrocities described, and that it referred almost exclusively to the treatment of Jewish, not political, prisoners. Since the majority of refugees in this country were Jews, this fact did not spoil their pleasure. By a little wishful thinking and a very free interpretation of this lone effort in government propaganda for Hitler's German victims they actually came to believe that official Britain was fraternising with them. They were soon to be disillusioned, not horribly and tragically, as would happen later, but insidiously: their will to work was fobbed off or looked at askance; and their first enthusiasm was chilled by the attitude of the authorities.

The War Office, the Ministry of Labour and the Aliens Department of the Home Office discussed the position of the refugees without advancing one step. Finally the critical state of the finances of the major relief organisations precipitated the issue at one point and official approval was given to recruit refugees into the Auxiliary Military Pioneer Corps and into the British Army as 'tradesmen' skilled in certain technical occupations, to get them off the pay-roll of the committees.

As soon as this was decided, male refugees of whatever profession between the ages of 18 and 50 who were maintained by the relief organisation were invited to join the Pioneer Corps. They had little choice since the recruiting office was run directly by the insolvent committee which would otherwise have had to support them. This recruiting policy completely ignored the War Office regulations for British subjects as regards call-up ages and reserved occupations, cases of hardship or conscientious objection, and fell between the two stools of conscription and voluntary enlistment by applying financial sanctions. That many of the refugees had reasonable chances of emigrating within a short time, that their visas would expire during their Army service, and they might not have another opportunity to obtain new visas, was given no consideration, and the policy of keeping men to clean out latrines at the expense of the government when they had a future assured overseas if they were allowed a few weeks' maintenance for their emigration plans to be completed, runs counter to common sense.

The superficial arguments were perfectly sound: the exiles had been given hospitality by a country now called upon to mobilise its entire resources for a major war. Hitherto the refugees had been madly seeking to comply with the instructions to re-emigrate; now they might remain in the United Kingdom. It was not too much to expect that they should seize this opportunity to prove their good faith towards the country that had granted them asylum by taking up arms in that country's defence.

It is a minor criticism to say that they were in fact permitted to take up not arms but scrubbing brushes and spades, nor is the waste of specialised talent and skill amongst refugees worth comment, since quite as much waste was observable amongst British experts in almost every sphere. That they were not to be allowed to take up arms was argued, correctly, to be entirely in their own interests and in deference to the fact that if they were in the front line, or liable to be captured, they would be treated as rebels and traitors and not as prisoners of war.

This fate, indeed, awaited and overtook the refugees in the Czechoslovak Army in France who were massacred between the Somme and the Marne in June 1940. This possibility, although obviously recognised by the leaders of the Czechoslovak Army operating under the Allied High Command, did not deter them from conscripting the Czechoslovak refugees in France into the Army as their only alternative to internment.

It is nevertheless plain that both refusing to arm the Austrian and German anti-Nazis and denying them the guarantees accorded to soldiers in wartime were reflections of the fact that they were not trusted or regarded as friends. They were simply thrown into a labour battalion to relieve the committees of financial responsibility for them. Their status was never properly defined. Their wives and children could look to no allowances, and they were not themselves assured of the right to return to or settle on British soil after demobilisation if they did not wish to go back to Central Europe. It must be made quite clear that, while the overthrow of the Hitler regime was a real issue to the refugees from Germany and Austria (a cause which had been theirs when British statesmen were shaking Hitler by the hand), the British government had not defined its war and peace aims. In this situation it is difficult to see how a man could be expected to view with enthusiasm the prospect of sacrificing his whole future in order to perform menial services to which he and his kind were certainly not essential since there were still a million-and-a-half British unemployed.[5] If the British government was not going to allow the refugee to settle on British territory after the war, then he was left with the personal duty of ensuring for his family some hope of settling elsewhere. His return to his country of origin was as problematic as the peace aims which had not been enunciated by Britain. The refugees who were now pressed into the Army included men who had a reasonable chance of emigrating to the United States, where the right to work awaited them; the surgeons and violinists and precision workers who were now set to dig holes saw the end of their hopes of ever being able to use their hands in their own profession again without so much as the consolation of knowing that after the war they would have the right to sing or sell matches in the streets of Britain.

2

An Order in Council of 17 November 1939, revoking the condition which forbade aliens to take work (and which was itself revoked by a subsequent order in July 1940), resulted in the employment of some 17,000 refugees between that date and May 1940.

Thus about 26 per cent of the total number of refugees did, in fact, find work despite the various disabilities under which they still suffered after the issue of the Order.

In effect the Order served the primary purpose of removing from the government the reproach that, at a time of military conscription, intensified demands on production and financial stringency, tens of thousands of aliens were, by government decree, permitted to live in idleness on British charity or public funds.

The Order had been in contemplation since the outbreak of war and had been foreshadowed then by the Home Secretary.[6] At the time it had been represented as an advantage to the country. The three months' delay, during which the status of the refugees had become more and more anomalous, gave the Order, when it was issued, a somewhat different character: it looked less like an effort to mobilise refugee skill and ability and more like an attempt to disarm criticism of government refugee policy.

There was, of course, an overwhelming case to be made for employing all available labour at the outset of a 'total' war, but it is a case that could have been made with greater justice in respect of our own unemployed. That some form of work should be exacted from every able-bodied man and woman at such a time would seem less unreasonable than that an untold number – apart from the registered and insured unemployed – should have been out of jobs. Yet such was the situation and the refugees, being a conspicuous element in the community distinguished by its high incidence of (enforced) unemployment, were liable to give more offence to public opinion than the mere waste of manpower spread over all sections of British labour.

The Order spelt genuine relief for the refugee committees bearing the impossible burden of maintenance, whereas the Czech Refugee Trust Fund, the one subsidised body, was in a highly vulnerable position insofar as it was spending Treasury funds to support the 'leisured' refugees.

It will be seen therefore that, as a diplomatic move, the November Order was inevitable. Something had to be done about the unemployed refugees and the time for internment was not yet ripe. Incidentally, it enabled 17,000 persons to feel again the satisfaction of being in work and to spend a few months in improving their skills and regaining their spirit before being interned.

Unfortunately the Order was not accompanied by any official propaganda to encourage the employment of refugee labour. This was a very material failure since it is clear that, for potential employers no less than for the refugee organisations and the refugees themselves, acceptance of the principle of refugee non-employment had become established over years of hard experience. Individual cases of refugees with special qualifications had been the subject of repeated and often vain applications and representations to the authorities. The process had been infinitely complicated and had entailed great persistence and patience, so if a vacancy had to be filled quickly employers could not look to refugee labour. The war had merely intensified these difficulties by the suspension of all new labour permits and the Order, issued three months too late, could not have revived the dampened spirits of potential employers unless the government had given wide publicity to its apparent change of policy. A mere stroke of the pen by one of His Majesty's Principal Secretaries of State could not by itself undo the careful conditioning of years.

The relief committees had similarly developed their work on quite different lines and were in no sense organised to function as agencies for putting refugees into the regular labour market. The various occupational and specialised committees had learned how to skirt around or crawl under the regulations; during the three months that had elapsed since the outbreak of war their ceaseless efforts to obtain a definite statement and a clarification of the position of the refugees had prevented them from embarking on any large-scale readjustment in preparation for the new ruling. It was, moreover, not until 17 November that the condition of 'temporary stay', on which the refugees had been allowed to land, was lifted by another Order.

From the end of November 1939 refugees were entered on a special supplementary register at their local Labour Exchanges. If no British subject was on the ordinary register to fill the requirements, the Labour Manager could turn to the supplement. No employer was able to take on a refugee except through the Labour Exchange, and in certain categories and special cases he had to make a direct application to the Ministry of Labour. The new provisions applied only to refugees who had passed through their tribunals and were freed from all restrictions[7] and to Czechoslovaks. Before sending a refugee for a job, the Labour Exchange had to ascertain from the prospective employer whether his firm was engaged in any form of Auxiliary War Service (in which case a special permit had to be obtained for the refugee) or such work as was 'scheduled' (prohibited to aliens) by the Order.[8] In the case of doctors and nurses the ban was absolute, since almost all hospitals and sanatoria had been absorbed into the Emergency Medical Scheme in readiness for such naval, military or air-force casualties as might occur. To these hindrances in obtaining employment must be added that of the language difficulty: thousands of the refugees did not speak English and none was familiar with our Labour Exchange procedure.

The relief organisations adjusted to the new demands with the flexibility born of their unswerving desire to help the refugees. Efforts were made to set up employment advisory and information centres and to use the provincial committees to liaise between refugees and local Labour Exchanges. These moves met with some, though not complete, success. The shift of emphasis from rescue work and pure relief work to questions of retraining and employment was too great to make for real efficiency in the early stages, while the qualifications for this new type of work were not forthcoming on demand. It was the same old story: large numbers of extraordinarily willing, humane and untrained persons were required, almost overnight, to master and implement government decrees without any of the necessary experience or machinery for doing so. Critics at a distance might aver that the new regulations were self-explanatory and that no help was needed in applying them; that the refugees had nothing more complicated to do than to register with their local Labour Exchanges and forfeit their right to support if they failed to do so. That was to ignore the fact that refugees were foreigners, many belonging to the professional classes, and if they were artisans qualified to work in war industries, they were prohibited from doing so.

Perhaps the most effective single factor in enabling refugees to make use of the permission to work was the organised representative body of the refugees themselves. Owing to their previous work, the various leaders of the refugee groups were in close touch with their members throughout the country and were familiar not only with their present circumstances but also with their previous occupational qualifications. If a member of a group found work in a particular trade or factory, he immediately reported the conditions and opportunities to the group leader, who was able to suggest to the central organisation that suitably qualified persons should be moved into those areas. The mobility of the refugees was a valuable asset and, thanks largely to the unofficial help the organised refugees gave to each other, the skilled industrial workers and artisans were gradually absorbed, many of them obtaining Auxiliary War Service permits.

While distinguished individual specialists in the technical and intellectual professions also obtained work, sometimes in government departments, the bulk of Jewish refugees from the liberal professions and the black-coated workers in industry and commerce remained unemployable so long as they were not retrained. Retraining itself was a considerable problem. It depended almost entirely upon private enterprise and private capital being sunk into workshops or suitable farming property. The government labour camps were not available for refugees and most of the technical schools and classes were reserved for British trainees in the Army.

As for agriculture, since the number of workers on the land had declined at the rate of 12,000 men a year between 1921 and 1937, with two million less arable acreage at the outbreak of this war than in 1914, it was soon realised that there would be an almost unlimited demand for agricultural labour. It was optimistically supposed that all refugees not otherwise employable would become unskilled farm workers and that they might play a fairly useful part in the government's ploughing-up schemes. Farmers and peasants from Slovakia, the Sudeten areas and Carpatho-Ruthenia were, indeed, speedily absorbed, as were those young people who had been retrained in this country for eventual emigration to Palestine. At that point, however, the back-to-the-land movement amongst refugees came to a virtual standstill. Men who were skilled workers, even though they could find no immediate openings, were very reluctant to lose their chance of being employed in their own trades and believed that by waiting they would find more suitable work.

More reluctant still, but with less justification, were the professional and commercial types of refugee, to whom agricultural labour represented a loss of social status. Here, if anywhere, the criticism that the refugees were not prepared to make sacrifices to benefit the people of Britain who had given them hospitality can be sustained; later, when some form of employment of national importance or use to the community became a possible, though by no means certain, alternative to internment, a marked change was observable in the attitude of these 'class-conscious' refugees and agriculture gained a number of recruits.

Forestry presented an equal opening with similar disadvantages for the refugees. It is to be noted, however, that large numbers of refugees with no previous experience in manual labour did in fact volunteer for both these occupations, and that many of them did so with the conscious wish to contribute to the welfare of the British people.

To sum up: the labour power of the refugees, theoretically released by the Order of November, was put to full use where this was possible, with the indispensable help of the relief organisations and their own fellow-refugees. No government department exerted itself to facilitate either the training or employment of refugees and no official spokesman encouraged employers to avail themselves of the intelligent and skilled labour which the refugees had to offer. As in the Army, so also in civilian life, it was plain that the refugees were regarded not as equals but as auxiliaries, tolerated because intolerance could not yet be justified.

All this time, with dwindling funds and a staff of workers largely inexperienced in employment problems, the relief organisations had the primary task of putting refugee life in Britain on a more settled and permanent basis, of arranging for more suitable forms of accommodation, of helping their protégés – too long accustomed to the assistance of an 'aid committee' – to become self-reliant as a first step to becoming self-supporting.

3

As a background to the practical re-orientation of refugee life there were certain political anomalies which could not fail to strike the refugees in the early days of the war.

For example, in September 1939, the RAF scattered leaflets over Germany in which the Austrian *Anschluß* and the cession of the Sudeten areas were referred to as examples of pacific arbitration. This confirmed that the foreign domination of those peoples was riveted upon them with British approval and set up two forms of disquiet: in the first place it suggested that yet further claims might have been settled by appeasement – a very grave shock to the democrats of all countries – and, secondly, it placed the anti-Nazi refugees from Austria and the Sudeten areas in the position of seeing a foreign power attempting to foreclose their fight for self-determination.

From when exactly was German aggression supposed to date? If on 3 September 1939, then Czechs and Slovaks were presumably in the same boat as Sudetens and Austrians. This, however, was not in accordance with official pronouncements, which reported with satisfaction (and great exaggeration) the figures of Czechoslovak nationals volunteering for the Czech Legion then being formed in France under the Allied Command. If, somewhat arbitrarily, the date could be fixed at 15 March 1939, this put Danzigers and Memellanders, as well as Czechs, on one side, with Sudeten-Germans and Austrians on the other. This spelt a re-division of Europe, the logic of which was mystifying to ordinary people, including the refugees who were most vitally affected by any such Allied war aims. It was very plain that their status in this country during the war would be conditioned by the British government's views on what should be the status of their respective countries after an Allied victory.

In France there was no beating about the bush: the entire body of male refugees (not excluding those Czechs of military age who did not join the Legion) was clapped into gaol at the outbreak of war and there were many here who sighed for a similar resolute handling of the problem and who, at precisely the juncture when the results of French internal policy seemed at their disastrous worst, got their way.[9]

In contradiction to the message of that first official leaflet, Sudeten Germans in Britain, in common with Czechs and Slovaks, were designated 'friendly aliens' – thus moving the date of Nazi aggression back to September 1938 – while Austrians, like Germans, were 'enemy aliens'. A few months later Danzigers were also listed as 'enemy aliens', thus giving recognition to Hitler's seizure of Danzig and again changing the date, this time to August 1939.

While indigenous Nazi movements had sprung up, led by Seyss-Inquart in Austria, by Henlein in the Sudeten areas and by Forster in Danzig, the Czech people (though they had their fascist traitors) had been united in their desire to resist Hitler and foreign domination. Was this, however, not equally true of every politically active Austrian from the illegal opposition? And had not the German opposition movements categorically denounced the subjugation of other countries by the Nazis? Why, then, were they to be considered less 'friendly' than the Czechs? If any such line of demarcation was valid, it could not logically be drawn between Austrians and Sudetens and between Sudetens and Danzigers, whose histories in relation to German Nazi rule were very similar. All three had entertained Nazi parties of a national character on their soil to pave the way for Hitler; all had produced a strong and courageous opposition to their own Nazi Party and its foreign backers, and from this opposition was derived a numerically small but important section of the refugees in Britain.

This geographical division of aliens merely produced absurdities and the arbitrary categories into which they were lumped had the ironical effect of going back on Munich, at a time when official propaganda still upheld it. Later, when the Czech National Committee was first formed, it forbore to include representatives of the 'friendly' Sudetens, an omission of which the misbegotten Czech National Government was also guilty.

As regards the non-political elements amongst the refugees, there could certainly not be much difference between the views of German Jews and Czech Jews (or between Austrian and Sudeten Jews) on the subject of Hitler. Nevertheless they were ruled to be friendly or inimical, to Britain, according to their territorial origins, except where these were confused by the authorities.[10]

These methods of approaching the delicate operation of separating the sheep from the goats amongst the refugees were not calculated to simplify the process, so the tribunals, whose task it was to do so, can hardly be blamed if, as happened in some cases, they applied tests as irrelevant and arbitrary as the original classifications.

In preparing the material for these tribunals, which started to function towards the end of September 1939, the British organisations for refugees drew on their voluminous *dossiers* on every individual case and filled out the rough-and-ready classifications which they had made at the Home Office's request immediately on, and in some cases before, the outbreak of war. Their material was invaluable but, owing to the confused methods of work by which a committee was often not informed that its registered cases were to appear until 24 hours before – and sometimes 24 hours after – the tribunal sitting, much of this documentation was wasted. The central organisation that collected and distributed the material from the separate committees for the use of the 28 tribunals in London and the 82 in other centres throughout the country had the superhuman task of discovering from the daily police lists of misspelled foreign names whether a certain Heinrich Cohn was one of the 500 or so of like name registered with the various Jewish organisations, with the Non-Aryans, with the Czechs, with the Catholics or with the Quakers, or whether he was not a refugee at all but merely a police-registered alien. When his identity had been established (and this could hardly ever be done without a shadow of doubt since no clues as to age or anything else were supplied by the police) the committee which had dealt with this particular Heinrich Cohn was expected to produce the relevant material. Sometimes the interval between receiving the original police list and the tribunal sitting was no more than a few hours.

Further confusion arose from police ignorance of the history and geography of Europe. Czechs and Sudeten Germans over the age of 21 had been born in the Austro-Hungarian Empire and were sometimes registered as Austrians so that, while the government's intention was that these refugees should not be examined by 'enemy alien' tribunals, they were nevertheless (and with the disadvantage of not having had their credentials submitted for this purpose by their committee) called to appear and, in some cases, put under police surveillance and subsequently interned as a result of their misregistration.

The one-man tribunals set up under barristers and judges were to act as direct agents of the Home Office[11] in sifting the evidence provided by the Aliens Department, by MI5, by Scotland Yard's Special Branch, by the local police force and by the refugee organisations on every individual enemy alien in the United Kingdom. For this purpose the tribunal presidents, who were persons of varying eminence in the legal profession but had in almost all cases hardly any knowledge of the political and social background of the refugees nor any experience of work amongst them to make up for this deficiency, were assisted by, on the one hand, a police secretary from the locality and, on the other, a liaison officer generally provided by one of the refugee committees. The police secretary was intended to provide evidence from the *dossiers* of the authorities, including the alien's own statements to the immigration officer on landing. The liaison officer, whose appointment in each case had been approved by the Home Office, acted as interpreter where that was necessary and, if he or she was in a position to do so, supplied further details regarding the personal history of the individual and supplemented the material already submitted by the responsible refugee organisation.

In London, where there were many thousands of refugees coming under the Jewish, Christian, Quaker, Trade Union, Student, Youth and other specialised central bodies or the Czech Refugee Trust Fund, the functions of the liaison officer who might be from one of these organisations, but could not be from all of them, were necessarily limited to those of interpreting and, if the presidents were willing to listen, explaining the circumstances surrounding refugees in general. In the provinces, on the other hand, the familiarity of the liaison officers from the local committees with the individual refugees enabled them to give a personal – and sometimes very subjective – account of their protégés.

Many of the presidents, recognising their own shortcomings with respect to the task of ruling on matters completely outside their province, welcomed the contributions from the liaison officers who, in a voluntary capacity, all day and for weeks on end, proved yet again the extraordinary devotion of individual members of the British public to the interests of the refugees and did their explanatory work with the more receptive presidents to some effect.

The police secretaries acted, in a sense, as a counter-weight (or 'counsels for the prosecution') to the liaison officers (in the main acting as 'counsels for the defence') and had as little background knowledge of refugees and their problems as the presidents – often less. They had a tendency to apply the clumsy yardstick of criminal practice to the refugees, viewing the histories of men and women who had been in concentration camps as 'a police record' and being hostile to those 'extremist' views which were in so many cases the precise reason why the alien had been granted asylum in this country. When this technique seemed too blunt for the trained minds of the presidents, they sought other sources of information if they were conscientious. In this way it occurred that presidents sometimes lent an ear to informants who were not always reliable among the refugees themselves and, being unaware of the whirlpools and cross-currents in refugee political struggles and intrigues, probably did more harm than good as a result of this one-sided information. Some of the judges, again, entertained an invincible prejudice against foreigners as such; others, with rugged individualism and overriding the carefully worded Home Office terms of reference, were stoutly convinced that general internment, as in the last war, was the only way to deal with aliens. It became necessary for the Home Office to supplement their detailed instructions to the presidents by calling them together at a meeting to explain that certain principles were involved and should be consistently observed.

The principles themselves were reasonable and did not allow much scope for individual presidents of tribunals who held private views on the treatment or general undesirability of aliens. 'Refugees from Nazi Oppression' were to be pronounced as such to distinguish them from all other types of aliens in the country. The instructions ruled that aliens who were known to have dubious connections or Nazi sympathies, or whose behaviour in this country had warranted reasonable suspicion, were to be listed in category 'A' and interned. They would have the right of appeal and an Advisory Committee was set up to deal with such appeals. A second 'B' category was for those refugees who failed to satisfy the tribunals of their absolute trustworthiness, but against whom nothing of a suspicious nature was known. Being placed in this category meant being put under police surveillance, forbidden to take employment and, among other restrictions, observing a 5-mile limit in accordance with the Order in Council made at the outbreak of war.[12] The third 'C' category entitled the refugees so listed to enjoy unrestricted freedom and they had only to observe the formalities common to all foreigners in this country, including Americans and Frenchmen.

Despite the provisions made and the repeated instructions given, there were grave misinterpretations. Refugees were listed 'A' and interned because, although they were recognised as having escaped from Nazi oppression and were not suspected of Nazi sympathies and connections, their left-wing politics evoked an ineradicable prejudice in some reactionary tribunal presidents.[13] There were refugees who were relegated to category 'B' on the principle that if nothing special was known against them, however much was known in their favour, the police had better watch them. On the other hand, a number of extremely shady characters with influential friends and ingratiating manners, as well as some highly placed German nationals who were not refugees from Nazi oppression, obtained 'C' certificates and a freedom of movement and action in apparent contradiction to the whole purpose of this winnowing process.

By the beginning of 1940, when the tribunals had finished their work, there were 573 'A' aliens, of whom well over a quarter were acknowledged 'Refugees from Nazi Oppression', 6,691 'B's and 64,324 'C's, of whom 13,000 individuals were not refugees at all. It was supposed that, apart from appeals against internment coming up slowly before the Advisory Committee and such cases where changed circumstances or suspicious behaviour warranted a review, the government had settled this aspect of the refugee problem for the duration of the war.

A good deal of discontent was felt both by the refugees themselves and by the organisations responsible for them concerning the number of 'B' rulings. The ban on employment represented a heavy burden on funds and, although 'B' refugees actually employed might continue in their work, the restriction on their movements and their perpetual visits to the police rendered them unsatisfactory employees. On an analysis of the rulings of the tribunals it was seen that certain judges had given 'B' rulings without any observable relevance to the merits of the cases. In view of this fact and the further evidence that some tribunals had revised this principle after the Home Office had reiterated its instructions, 'B' cases who had been so classified in the early days of the tribunals were allowed to appeal on grounds of hardship and were accorded 'C' rulings. Such appeals, however, were wholly dependent upon the refugee being aware of his rights in the matter (which, if he had lost touch with his committee on entering gainful employment before the tribunals sat, was unlikely), upon the claim for revision being supported by a responsible citizen or organisation and, lastly, upon his learning of the possibilities open to him before the local tribunals had ceased to sit. Once these bodies were dispersed such a review became a practical impossibility, entailing a long drawn-out and elaborate process to persuade the authorities to reconsider an individual case.

To appreciate fully the difficulty facing the tribunals it is necessary to anticipate the nature of the charges subsequently brought against the refugees. In the first place, the tribunals were not to know that the words 'refugee' and 'Fifth Columnist' were later to figure in the official vocabulary as synonyms. Secondly, while any trained English lawyer who is not blinded by prejudice is a fair judge of a witness's veracity and good faith, he is not necessarily competent to size up and attach due weight to the views and actions of people who have taken part in the illegal anti-fascist movements of Central Europe. To equate the underground opposition, with its dangers, its code of self-discipline and its heroism, to the underworld of crime, as the police secretaries did, was an error into which few of the presidents fell; but, unless they had some acquaintance with the background and circumstances of these active anti-Nazi fighters, they were at a loss. The other difficulty – that of knowing what they were supposed to be looking for – applied to the Jews and the politicals equally. Had the presidents understood that the then Home Secretary would disapprove of aliens who 'still have material interests in Germany'[14] they would possibly not have taken so lenient a view of the propertied and cultured aliens who had left Germany in the early 1930s with their interests there intact, before any laws and restrictions had been imposed; but a similar stigma attaches to a large number of notable and respected men in British financial and business circles to this day and no one dreams of arresting or deporting them on the grounds that their material interests might render them 'subject to pressure which would lead them, perhaps at the hour of our greatest peril, to take action, on an impulse it may be, which afterwards they might greatly regret'.[15] That argument, in any case, would apply with greater force to the many English people who lived in Germany by their own choice until the outbreak of war and who had property and businesses there, but no investigation of these men was instituted at all.

Again, how could the presidents guess that it would subsequently be ruled that, because refugees were employed on important work, they were *ipso facto* to be regarded as more trustworthy – the last category to be interned and among the first categories to be released – than the unemployed, of whom there were infinitely larger numbers at the time when the tribunals sat than at the internment period. This can only have been on the theory that an enemy agent can do his work better living on the dole in a refugee hostel than if he is in a key position in British industry or Auxiliary War Service.[16]

Certainly, if one anticipates the somewhat eccentric view taken of the types of refugee likely and unlikely to be a danger to this country, the work of the tribunals appears very wide of the mark, but the task was, frankly, beyond the powers of the presidents who fulfilled the terms of their instructions in many cases faithfully, in more cases inadequately, and, in a few, not at all, according to their personal ability to handle matters completely outside their knowledge and to detach themselves from their preconceived views on politics and on aliens.

In accordance with the Home Secretary's announcement immediately on the outbreak of war, a special tribunal had been set up to examine the cases of Czechoslovak refugees. As this tribunal was a centralised body functioning not merely as an agent of the Home Office (as were the Enemy Alien Tribunals) but under the aegis of that government department, its nature and procedure were not generally known to the public and, apart from an occasional mention in the press, it received no publicity. Nor, of course, were its cases, which concerned officially Friendly Aliens, the subject of public alarm or hostility, or even of much interest, and it will be understood that any reference to the possibly doubtful character of Czechoslovak refugees would have awakened strong protest, as was evidenced at the very first mention of the subject:

> Sir J. Anderson: I am also arranging for a similar review, by a special tribunal, of all Czechs-Slovaks. Citizens of the former republic of Czecho-Slovakia will not be treated as enemy aliens –
>
> Mr. Dalton: This is reparation for Munich.
>
> Sir J. Anderson: – although there may be amongst them certain individuals who will be subjected to restrictions similar to those applicable to enemy aliens.[17]

So the examination of these refugees, which did not require their attendance in person, was soft-pedalled. This is unfortunate, for this special tribunal constituted the sanest and most intelligent method of examination adopted, since it was conducted by a president who had a wide knowledge of the refugees' country of origin and an intimate acquaintance with their national background, their internal political structures, and their complicated domiciliary laws by which so many of the refugees' credentials could be tested.[18]

The material furnished to this tribunal came from much the same sources as that for the enemy alien tribunals – that is to say, all official information with additional and corroborative matter supplied by the Czech Refugee Trust Fund.

The later arrest of certain Czechoslovak subjects under the Aliens Order, as amended by the Defence Regulations, was carried out by administrative order a few days before the recognition of the émigré Czechoslovak government in Britain. The matter of aliens (other than enemy aliens) detained under these regulations was raised in the House of Commons with the request that these cases should be investigated by a tribunal. In his reply the then Home Secretary made it plain that he was satisfied that these cases merited the present alternative to deportation (namely imprisonment) without further investigation.

Czechoslovaks (other than criminals) so arrested formed a special category insofar as no charges were brought against them. Their crime was that they represented elements in this country opposed to the émigré Czech government formed with British approval. These arrests may have indicated that this self-appointed body required the protection of the British authorities from the criticism of its own nationals but there is, of course, no reason to suppose that the Czech Tribunal was party to this singular discrimination.

4

From January to May 1940 the position of the refugees deteriorated steadily.

There were two major moves in this period that affected them adversely. First, there was the scaling-down of maintenance allowances, introduced by the Czech Refugee Trust Fund, the one body endowed by the government, and the voluntary organisations, now receiving government aid on a pound-for-pound basis, which adopted Unemployment Assistance Board scales and procedures. Second, a further system of tribunals was set up to review all 'B' cases and such 'C' cases as were open to doubt, and to consider the position of refugees living in the eight 'Protected Areas' listed in March.

The new tribunals consisted of 12 Regional Committees and were presided over by a legal chairman (in most cases a County Court judge). The members consisted of half a dozen local dignitaries – JPs, Aldermen and suchlike – a police secretary (generally an Inspector from the County Police Headquarters) and in almost every case an Admiralty representative (a naval or naval reserve officer of high rank). Liaison officers were again appointed by the local refugee committees and were approved by the Home Office as for the previous tribunals.

Like the former examinations, these new tribunals were able to accept information other than evidence in the legal sense and their discretion in sifting and interpreting this evidence was paramount. Since no one but the liaison officer – now heavily outclassed – was in any sense acquainted with refugee problems and the complicated circumstances surrounding the case of the political refugee in particular (in which the route taken to emigrate or the date at which a passport was issued may signify a great deal more than any police evidence of, or private testimony to, his reliability), it was plain that these Regional Advisory Committees could not be expected to sort out the trustworthy from the untrustworthy. What exactly they existed for, except as a sop to anti-refugee opinion in the War Office, is not known, nor does it greatly matter, since the Regional Committees had not covered more than 25 per cent of their cases when the internment drive intervened and the programme was called off.

What does matter, however, is the attitude implicit in the establishment and composition of these fresh tribunals. For the first time the Service departments and their police took an open hand in refugee questions. With this transfer of control, government policy emerged sharply from the hazes and hesitations of civil administration.

Two hundred refugees who had no alternative accommodation were arrested in the Protected Areas as a foretaste of what was to come.

The reduction of the maintenance allowances also confirmed

that the status of refugees was rapidly declining. That this move was not owing to lack of funds was proved by the fact that the Czech Refugee Trust Fund, the one rich and subsidised body, led the way and was the first to introduce the cuts.

There were many arguments to justify bringing the refugees – now permitted to work – into line with the British unemployed, so long as they had the same chances of getting jobs. Some people sympathetic to the refugees and having, in the course of their work, made good friends with men and women of their own class amongst refugees, had never been and were not now able to recognise that a refugee, whatever his former position or status, is a refugee and that by no manner of means is it possible to reinstate him completely in his country of exile.[19] Just as professionals and businessmen were reduced, from the start, to a standard of living far below that to which they had been accustomed and were uprooted from their interests, so the political refugees were also cut off from the proper sphere and mainspring of their lives. Each in his way suffered deprivations as bitter as they were inevitable and no amount of charity and benevolence can compensate for the tragedies attendant upon exile. When that is understood there is still a vast difference between depressing the refugees to the lowest subsistence level, making paupers and beggars of them, and attempting to rehabilitate lives broken through no fault of their own and still of infinitely precious social value. Under the new system of reduced maintenance the refugees, nearly three-quarters of whom did not find work, were driven in their voiceless numbers into more sordid surroundings, with fewer freedoms and less opportunity for interest and recreation. Elderly men who had lived too long in the world of middle-class standards to relinquish them completely spent their allowance on fresh linen and shoe repairs, finding their food and warmth by sitting for hours on end over a cup of coffee in a tea-shop. Bus fares, shoe repairs and even newspapers became luxuries. If there was the chance of a job, men with high-grade qualifications could not present themselves in clothes bought on a two-shillings-a-week allowance and could not even save enough on food to clothe themselves in a manner befitting their professional status.

It is not these hardships that should excite pity for the refugees but the fact that, while population after population was decimated and its finest flower betrayed and massacred, British officialdom was working out methods of harassing, quizzing, restricting, humiliating and degrading the handful of staunch spirits who had escaped from fascist countries. That, indeed, is a pitiable thing.

NOTES

1. To quote one typical and early example:

    This present emergency differs from the Great War of 1914–18 in two particulars. In the first place, broadly speaking, during the previous War all the subjects of Germany and Austria, and the other Powers allied against us, were potential enemies, whereas of course ... it is evident that there are resident in this country many persons who are technically enemy subjects and are more enthusiastically with us in the prosecution of the war than anyone else. (Mr Pethick-Lawrence, House of Commons, 4 September 1939 (*Official Report*, Vol. 351, cols 405–6))

2. The plans prepared are based on the principle that effective steps must be taken to render harmless all aliens who may be hostile to this country, but that there should be no unnecessary interference with other foreigners, of whom many are anxious to help this country ... A large proportion of these Germans and Austrians at present in this country are refugees, and there will, I am sure, be a general desire to avoid treating as enemies those who are friendly to the country which has offered them asylum. (Sir John Anderson, Home Secretary, House of Commons, 4 September 1939 (*Official Report*, Vol. 351, cols 366–7))
3. Cmd. 6120, *Papers Concerning the Treatment of German Nationals in Germany, 1938–1939.*
4. These documents were not written for publication, and, indeed, so long as there was the slightest prospect of reaching any settlement with the German Government it would have been wrong to do anything to embitter relations between the two countries. (Introduction, Cmd. 6120)
5. 1,395,550 on 11 September 1939, and 1,477,586 on 13 November 1939.
6. I am anxious that use shall be made of the help of friendly aliens in any direction in which their assistance may be advantageous to this country. For this purpose I am in consultation with the Minister of Labour as to the manner in which use can be made of the services of aliens who are not at present at liberty to take employment. I hope it may be possible to arrange that aliens who are friendly to this country may be found employment through the Employment Exchanges. (Sir John Anderson, House of Commons, 4 September 1939 (*Official Report*, Vol. 351, cols 367–8))
7. See below.
8. SCHEDULE:
    1. Employment in any prohibited place within the meaning of the Official Secrets Act, 1911, as subsequently amended, or in any protected place within the meaning of Regulation 12 of the Defence Regulations, 1939.

2. Employment in the manufacture, construction, supply, repair, testing or maintenance of arms, explosives, ammunition, ships, vehicles or aircraft intended for the use of, or used by, His Majesty's forces, or in any factory or other premises where such manufacture, construction, supply, repair, testing or maintenance as aforesaid is carried out or directed.
3. Employment in any radio, telegraph or telephone company engaged in the transmission of naval, military or air force messages.
4. Employment in any railway company or in any other company engaged in the provision of transport for His Majesty's forces by sea or land.
5. Employment in any naval, military or air force hospital or in any other hospital providing treatment for His Majesty's forces.
6. Employment in any canteen, club or institute of a social, benevolent or religious character conducted wholly or partly for the benefit of members of his Majesty's forces or in any organization of a like character and with a like purpose if the employment may involve contact or correspondence with members of His Majesty's forces.
7. In this Schedule the expression 'company' includes any person or body of persons, whether incorporated or not.

9. Then there was the collapse of France, profoundly altering the military problems which confront us in this country. On 21 June, after the fullest and most earnest consideration the policy of general internment was decided upon. (Sir John Anderson, House of Commons, 22 August 1940 (*Official Report*, Vol. 364, col 1545))
10. A considerable number of Czech and Sudeten refugees were registered as Austrians and Germans by the police.
11. To avoid risks, I propose that, to supplement the information already in my possession, there shall be an immediate review of all Germans and Austrians in this country, and I am asking a number of men with legal experience to assist me in this matter. (Sir John Anderson, House of Commons, 4 September 1939 (*Official Report*, Vol. 351, col 367))
12. The new Order requires all enemy aliens (that is, Germans and Austrians) who are over the age of 16 and do not intend to leave the country at once, to report to the police, and provides that they must obtain police permits for change of residence, for travelling, and for the possession of certain articles, including cameras and motor cars. (Sir John Anderson, House of Commons, 4 September 1939 (*Official Report*, Vol. 351, cols 366–7))
13. For example, it sometimes happened that the refugee was asked if he would be prepared to take up arms against the Soviet Union, then a party to the Soviet–German Non-Aggression Pact, and if he said he was not, he was automatically included in category 'A' as hostile.
14. Sir John Anderson, House of Commons, 22 August 1940 (*Official Report*, Vol. 364, col 1546).
15. Ibid.
16. If they are dangerous, in the first place, how is it that, under one of the categories, those people who occupy key positions are to be released? … If they are dangerous, keep them in; if they are not dangerous, let them out; and if you do not know whether they are dangerous or not, put them in key positions, where they are able to do any amount of damage!

(Colonel Wedgwood, House of Commons, 22 August 1940 (*Official Report*, Vol. 364, col 1563))

17. House of Commons, 4 September 1939 (*Official Report*, Vol. 351, col 367).
18. Sir Ronald Macleay, KCMG.
19. This plea for class distinctions to be observed has even been extended to internment camp conditions:

> Similarly, although I know it is almost impossible to make discriminations as to comforts within these camps, I cannot but think that there are cases of persons of real eminence formerly in their own country, cases of very distinguished people who might be allowed a little more latitude in the way of personal comfort than is perhaps required by the great mass of the interned. (The Lord Archbishop of Canterbury, House of Lords, 5 September 1940 (*Official Report*, Vol. 117, col 385))

Of course, the great mass of the interned had, in their own country, at one time enjoyed an eminence above a palliasse on the floor.

The Right of Asylum Lost

Significance of anti-refugee campaign – Internment – Deportations – Releases

1

The campaign against the refugees is thought by many people to have been started by certain sections of the press in the middle of April 1940 and to have reached its peak in reflecting the popular clamour for their internment by the first fortnight in May, at which stage the government gave way.

This theory of spontaneous generation must be entirely discarded. The opening shots of the anti-refugee campaign were not fired by the papers which headlined the 'alien menace'; these merely followed a lead given by the establishment of the revision tribunals in March 1940 which ordered the internment of over 300 people graded 'B' or 'C' by the former tribunals. This represented a policy recommended, if not actually initiated, by Military Intelligence and the War Office. The policy was made explicit by a group of Tory MPs who formed a deputation to the Home Secretary in April; so the newspaper campaign of about the same date, in reflecting this, comes fairly low in the list of causality.

Sir John Anderson (the then Home Secretary) has said:

> The first significant step was taken on 11th May after Norway had been overrun and when the attack had already been launched on Holland and Belgium. The military authorities came to me, late one evening, and represented that, in view of the imminent risk of invasion, it was in their view of the utmost importance that every male enemy alien between 16 and 70 should be removed forthwith from the coastal strip which in their view was the part of the country likely, if invasion took place, to be affected. I listened to the representations of the military authorities and came to the conclusion that it was quite impossible to reject the case put before me. I accepted their suggestion and carried

> it into force within 24 hours. I invited representatives of the Press to meet me, so that I might explain what had happened. I explained how deeply I regretted the necessity for the step. Hon. Members might like to look back at the Press of Monday, 13th May – I saw the representatives on the Saturday – and see the line that was taken then. The hon. Member for Westhoughton was challenged in various quarters when he said the Press with one voice called for the internment of all enemy aliens. I think perhaps he put it a bit high. But there was not a responsible newspaper on 13th May who did not applaud what had been done.[1]

It is interesting to contrast the Home Secretary's frank exposition of the sequence of events – military representations, Home Office action, press conference, subsequent press campaign – with his Under-Secretary's version six weeks before:

> Throughout the winter and until early May we were able, with some support in this House, to resist the clamour to 'intern the lot'.[2]

It is a matter for wonderment that Colonel Wedgwood, to cite but one individual, should fancy the Home Office 'too easily swayed by the *Daily Mail* and by the agitation of uneducated, panicky people',[3] and for satisfaction that Sir John Anderson, in the passage cited above, should have disposed of that fancy.

As far as public opinion goes, various pilot surveys were made by such bodies as the British Institute of Public Opinion and Mass Observation, whose findings and comments have been published, but while they profess that the Fifth Column news from Holland was an important factor in swaying public opinion against refugees in May, they fail to explain why, before June was out, when the Fifth Column bogey had been greatly reinforced by the events in France and was given much support by the 'Silent Column'[4] campaign, then at its height, there should have been an almost universal outcry against the wholesale internments that had taken place. Moreover, it should be noted that the question put by the British Institute of Public Opinion in making its survey a day or two before 11 May (by a strange coincidence) referred to the treatment of 'Germans and other foreigners [*sic*]', which words, it is known, evoke a different association in most people's minds from the word 'refugees'. Nor was it 'other foreigners' who were removed from the coastal strip and interned – a point of some importance in accepting the case put before the Home Secretary by the military authorities.

Further, we should reflect upon the fact that, in bowing to public clamour – as the government would have us think they did – to 'intern the lot', it was by no means 'the lot' whom they interned.

The Hohenzollern princes and Prince Starhemberg were sufficiently notable exceptions to the general round-up for their continued freedom to have gained some publicity; lesser personages of the same type – not, it is fair to say, notable for their anti-fascist leanings – shared that freedom in modest obscurity. In reply to the parliamentary question of why an Italian fascist club in London was permitted to carry on its activities, the then Home Secretary stated that the club was 'already being watched'. This was on 22 August, ten weeks after the internment of Italians began, although Sir John Anderson has himself described the swiftness with which his Department was able to act where dangerous aliens were concerned. Pressed further as to what he proposed to do 'regarding the prominent Italian Fascists who are active in London while anti-Fascists are being arrested', Sir John replied that the internment of all Italians known to be members of the Italian Fascist Party had been ordered on the outbreak of war with Italy. The following interchange then took place:

Sir J. Anderson: If my hon. Friend knows of any others who have escaped notice, I should be glad if he would let me have particulars ...
Mr. Ammon: Has not the right hon. Gentleman already admitted this morning that the Fascist Club in Greek Street exists? It cannot exist without membership?
Sir J. Anderson: I said that it was being watched.[5]

Thus, despite the sufferings of 30,000 refugees, the British people were protected from the dangers presented by possible enemy agents which the internment policy claimed to meet.

If a large percentage of the population clamoured for the internment of refugees at a period which coincided precisely with a similar demand being pressed by the military authorities, a number of Tory MPs and an Anderson-inspired press, one may take it that this popular desire was fathered by these reactionary sections of the community and mothered by ignorance. While individuals who were unable to distinguish between fascists and anti-fascists gave free and well-publicised utterance to their prejudices and fears,[6] government officials, though better informed, remained discreetly silent and Mr Peake's attempts 'to resist the clamour' were represented as a lone effort in high-minded tolerance which found no echo in the people.[7]

The fact is that the internment policy adopted in May, and loyally supported by the press at the time, was scarcely modified and in no whit revised in the course of the subsequent months, but public approval was markedly absent from its sordid and ignominious application.

In tracing the origins and purposes of this policy it is impossible to find the slightest corroboration for the idea that it was the will of the British public. The press campaign which preceded the official internment policy is to be understood as a kite flown to test the reactions of the least-informed sections of the community, while there is much to suggest that the swift and wholesale manner in which the measure was put into effect was the long-delayed triumph of very deliberate, very dangerous and very reactionary policies, whose presence has never been wholly obscured throughout the refugee era.

The widely disseminated fiction of a sensible, kind but muddled government losing its head on the aliens question one fine day in May 1940 is a wild travesty. Certainly, for the individual, it makes a fundamental difference whether he is free or interned. However narrow, mean and dependent his liberty has been, confinement behind barbed wire under military guard, separated from his family and in conditions bereft of even the minimum amenities is, of course, a vast change. It is, however, ludicrous for the objective onlooker to interpret the government move as a reversal of previous policy and a momentary aberration. Or is it not? Has this interpretation helped the government or the refugees? Has it brought about a radical change in the internment policy, or has it enabled the government to maintain that policy while making countless small concessions?

Since 1933 the government allowed no refugees to obtain asylum in this country unless somebody else paid for it. The government was so fearful of arousing xenophobia in the British public, which was solely responsible for bringing the foreigners here at great expense to itself, that it dared not let them take employment. The government could not possibly influence the Dominions to open their doors to refugees (except, later, to accept 17,000 of them as prisoners).

Suddenly, on 11 May 1940, that wayward, impulsive body, the British government, in a momentary flutter of confusion, changed this policy of unrelieved parsimony and obstruction to one of persecution.

2

Before 11 May 1940, 929 enemy aliens had been interned – 573 by order of the first tribunals – and 50 had been released.

On 11 May, 3,000 German and Austrian males between the ages of 16 and 60 living on the 20-mile coastal belt scheduled as a 'Defence Area' were arrested and interned.

On 16 May a further 2,500 males from all over the country who had been placed in category 'B' by the tribunals were rounded up, including 16-year-olds who had reached this age since the tribunals had ceased sitting in January and who were automatically classed as 'B' on registering with the police, while 'C' category refugees living in newly scheduled areas were given the alternative of moving away or being interned. Many of them who had jobs in these areas were interned without the opportunity of trying to find work elsewhere.

On 28 May, 3,500 women in category 'B' were separately arrested and separately interned. In the first week of June, the upper age limit for internment was raised to 70.

On 3 June restrictions which had hitherto applied only to 'B' cases were extended to 'C' aliens and, as more areas became 'protected', further internments were ordered. These areas were no longer confined to coastal regions. No one knew which places would be proscribed next; for military reasons this information was withheld from the refugee organisations who were unable to provide alternative arrangements overnight for their protégés without running the risk of moving them from yesterday's protected areas into tomorrow's.

On 22 June (the day when the Franco-German Armistice was signed in the Forest of Compiègne), the general internment of the remaining 'C' refugees started, the unemployed being taken first, which included those who had lost their jobs on being ordered to leave coastal and other prohibited areas.

Some 3,100 Italians were also interned between 10 June and 22 June and, while members of the Fascist Party were supposed to be rounded up in this drive, the policy was to arrest Italian nationals who had not been domiciled in this country for 20 years or more – including all the anti-fascists who had fled from Italy since the early days of the fascist regime.[8] By August some 30,000 refugees had been interned under these orders

* * *

The internment policy thus initiated on 11 May, in circumstances clearly described by Sir John Anderson, virtually gave the refugees the status of prisoners of war, with the difference that they were considerably less well fed, that there was no one anywhere to protect their interests and that an invasion by the Nazis would mean their speedy release by massacre.

The 'get them out before it is too late' plea of Lord Baldwin, voiced when he launched his fund for the refugees after the pogroms in 1938, was now changed to 'lock them up before it is too late'; but whereas the earlier slogan made sense and British people responded by subscribing large sums of money to save the refugees from the persecution, torture and death which hung over them, it was very difficult for the same people to understand who was to be saved and from what by the incarceration of the refugees whom they had previously been asked to rescue.

These internments were not undertaken for the welfare of the refugees (although even this suggestion has been made in all seriousness)[9] but ostensibly for that of the country. It was at no time represented as a penal or retributive measure. The British government did not profess to believe, as the Hitler government did, that these Jews and anti-Nazis had in fact plotted or committed crimes against the State. It did not suggest that their very presence was a blot upon the national honour, nor yet that they were of a lower species detrimental to the community that they contaminated. Nevertheless, without claiming the least justification for so doing, this government treated them as criminals and sub-humans.

By what right, in order to preserve some chimera of the safety of the State, did the government condemn sick, dying and old refugees to sleep on thin palliasses or on bare, wet floors, with verminous blankets in tents under the rain, in damp wharfs and disused mills, in stables with leaking roofs?

What cynical contempt for the sufferings of Hitler's victims allowed the British government to confine together proven Nazi agents and the refugees from Nazi oppression: the persecuted and their persecutors?

In the name of what quality of justice and common humanity were men separated from their wives and mothers from their sons, sometimes in neighbouring camps, without leave to visit, and with correspondence held up for 14 days, while others, who had completed their arrangements for orderly re-emigration to countries where freedom and work awaited them, were held against their will, their papers lost and their identities confused?

What can excuse the fact that these refugees, against whom no charge was brought, were hauled from their lodgings by police in the early hours of the morning, without notice, given no time to collect their possessions, and carted off shamefully in prison vans to camps where they were unable to soften the shock to their families by communicating their whereabouts when they reached the camps? One hundred thousand letters addressed by the internees to their relatives were found at one time to have accumulated, undelivered, in the postal censor's office. Small wonder that those outside became frantic with distress; more so when it became known that of the 600 or 700 boys and girls interned upon their 16th birthday, the majority had been transhipped, and yet the mothers had no word telling them where their children might be.

The unhappy exiles, who had committed no offences against Britain, who had brought upon it no disgrace, and who had not added to its burdens or deserved its hatred, were kept behind barbed wire to be stared at by the public like beasts at the zoo, in water-logged camps without washing facilities, their papers and money confiscated; they were sent to their quarters when air-raid warnings sounded and told they would be shot if they emerged.

Old people and children, tubercular patients and diabetics, incurable invalids who could only survive by the constant care of their families, men who had fought at Dunkirk, the brains and the muscles and the unbroken spirit which had defied Hitler, all were flung to rot in the ill-equipped and unprepared camps.

There are English men and women who, out of their cold and

empty hearts and addled heads, defend this treatment of the refugees, but for the majority of the British people the shame of such acts committed in their name will want a lot of wiping out.

Apart from the vile conditions which nothing can ever excuse, the internment policy itself was completely unjustified by the fear of invasion. In every successive country coming under Nazi control – Austria, Czechoslovakia, Poland, Norway, Denmark, Belgium, Holland – the refugees, far from aiding the invader, had been the first victims of the Gestapo. So, while 1,000 political refugees were being executed in Holland and the remaining 7,000 from the four internment camps were sent to the plague spots of Dachau and Buchenwald, while the Gestapo was in the act of taking over the French government's refugee camps in Ambleteuse, Nevers, Dijon, Cepoy, Damigny, Gray and Paris, the British government embarked upon the last and wholesale phase of the internment drive – for fear of invasion.

A truly horrible analogy springs to mind. When the Nazis came to power over a disunited and humiliated people, they sought and found a good all-round scapegoat that had stood the test of time. It did not require much ingenuity to hit upon the Jews as the cause of all the wrongs the German people had suffered since 1914, and the thing caught on. If even 600,000 persons (the total number of German Jews) had to suffer in the process of rehabilitating the 65 million Germans (and canalising off their hatred and discontents) it was not too high a price to pay. The Jews were a danger to the German people; traitors who owed no allegiance to the country where they lived; even if one knew a decent Jew, that was not to be regarded as an exception, but merely as an instance of the cunning with which Jews could deceive simple, honest folk.

The British government did not use the same terms of abuse, merely the same arguments to justify their internment policy: in Germany they were Jews; in Britain they were Germans. The analogy is made more hideous by the fact that it was the same Jews who were interned – and on the same grounds: 'preventive custody.'[10]

It will be objected that the danger from the Jews in Germany was trumped up by unscrupulous propagandists for their own ends whereas the dangers of invasion in June 1940 in Britain were real. That argument, of course, will not stand. The dangers of invasion might be real, but it was from the refugees that the danger was supposed to come in the event of an invasion. To substantiate that charge, it would have to be shown that the refugee community harboured, unknown to the authorities, a number of actual or potential Nazi agents who were indistinguishable from genuine refugees. It would also have to be shown that, where countries had been invaded, it was the German and Austrian racial and political refugees who aided their capitulation. So far, although any such evidence would have been a godsend to the government in defending their case, none has been forthcoming.

In France, where the most flagrant betrayal of the French people occurred, it cannot have been the refugees from Nazi oppression who brought it about since they were safely, as some would phrase it, in internment camps and prisons. Others may be of the opinion that the true France would have been safer if the refugees and other anti-fascist elements had not been stowed away at this momentous testing-time. Be that as it may, the refugees who are loosely referred to as part of the Fifth Column may have been among the French (or the Belgian or the Dutch) war refugees crowding the roads. It is not suggested that they were, and the wisdom of looking for traitors among those homeless, terrified hordes of fleeing people is doubtful; but that they were among the refugees from Germany and Austria is a physical impossibility.

The reversal of refugee policy in France was part and parcel of the Munich Agreement policy which laid the basis for the complete sell-out of France to fascism. The fascist forces, working in the dark and for four years kept in check by a strong anti-fascist people's movement, were triumphant at Munich and emerged into the open. The victims of Munich – the refugees from Czechoslovakia – were not welcomed to France. The refugees already there were from that moment increasingly harassed and restricted. Illegal entry over the German border was now met with compulsion to work in a labour corps while expulsions from French territory multiplied. The refugee advisory bodies working under government aegis were disbanded. 'Foreign associations', by which was meant all organised bodies of refugees, came under strict and unsympathetic control. The scandal of the concentration camps for Spanish Republicans and International Brigaders, rotting in earth-holes and beaten up by Senegalese guards – again, part and parcel of the non-intervention policy – stank in the nostrils of the whole civilised world. The declaration of the 'anti-Nazi' war by the French appeasers and Non-Interveners was accompanied by the wholesale internment of all the remaining anti-fascist refugees.

On the evening of 1 September 1939 the Paris *Garde Mobile* raided and searched a large number of houses and arrested German and Austrian political refugees, who were taken to La Santé prison. From then on arrests were continuous and, by November, 30,000 arrests had been made. The Paris refugees, at first herded into the Colombes Stadium, were drafted into seven newly opened concentration camps. The refugee relief organisations were closed down, their committee members manhandled, and their funds confiscated. Czechs and Sudetens were also arrested and the Czech House of Culture, opened in August 1939 under the patronage of the French government, was also closed, while the famous Library of the Burned Books was impounded and partially destroyed.

By February 1940, there were 30 concentration camps. By March, of the 14,000 Austrians originally interned, 300 had enlisted in the French Legion, while 400 had been released on the grounds of advanced age, serious illness or because they had French relatives. An inter-ministerial investigation had decided upon 500 further releases, but only 50 of these were effected since the condition for release was some form of auxiliary war service. A hundred Austrians had been transferred to a labour camp in Damigny with interned Nazis.

The majority of refugee writers and artists were confined at Vernet under Senegalese guards with whips and a commandant who was an active member of the royalist *Action Française*. The prisoners' hair was cropped and they were provided with no blankets or mattresses, while at another camp, at Francillon-près-Blois, the internees lived in a cellar under a stable, considerably worse off than the horses above their heads. In the Meslay-du-Maine camp, where 2,000 Austrian refugees from the Paris district were confined, there were no washing facilities at all.

In the women's camp at Uzuche, where young children were also imprisoned, no form of heating was provided until Christmas 1939, and the underfed children (8½ litres of milk for 110 of them) died of cold there. There were women of 15 nationalities, including young mothers and the wives of men condemned to life imprisonment or already murdered by the Gestapo.

The prisoners whose status was not defined in any way, save that generically the refugee population – poets, actors, writers, International Brigaders – was classed as undesirable, were not the subject of a single decree. Their fate was in the hands of the individual commandants of each camp. They were set to chopping wood and breaking stone and to the heaviest unskilled work in the fields. Aid from the French population had almost ceased by January 1940 owing to its own hardships.

With the capitulation of France[11] the fate of the refugees was sealed and the Gestapo lost no time in combing through the camps in fulfilment of Article 19 of the Armistice.[12]

In the spring of 1941 it became known that 20 prominent German political refugees, including the former Social Democratic leader Breitscheid and the Social Democratic ex-Finance Minister Hilferding, who had been in unoccupied France and released for re-emigration, had been handed over to the German authorities by Pétain and returned to Germany. Similarly, Italian anti-fascists were handed over to the Italian government.

Those who were close to the refugee problem in France could trace in the gradual worsening of the conditions for refugees between September 1938 and September 1939 the hand of those anti-democratic forces which in the end triumphed over a far stronger people's movement than has been mobilised in Britain. In France, those who protested against the growing restrictions on refugees following Munich (which, in effect, reduced them to the position which they had all along occupied in this country) were unable to point the bitter moral as we can do and, with the outbreak of war, those protesting voices were themselves silenced.

Before final disaster engulfed France, democratic institutions and civil liberties had been swept away, and we know that these are not the symbols but the very air of freedom, without which great nations suffocate, are strangled in the dark and die.

Step by step, the victories won by the French people (during the same period which distinguished France for its generous treatment of the refugees) were wrested from them and at each successive stage the plea of 'national security and strength' was advanced. Does anyone believe today that these steps were taken with a view to ensuring a strong and secure France for its people? Does anyone believe that they were so many 'stupid mistakes'?

Politicians are not above average stupidity, nor do they rise to power on a capacity for blundering into mistakes any normally intelligent person would avoid. France was not ruled by helpless fools when it was party to the Hoare–Laval plan, the non-intervention policy and the Munich Agreement. There is no room for a pitying tolerance of the errors of politicians: they know full well what they are doing and do it because their aims and purposes are not those of the people.

The internment of the refugees in France, though it served no other purpose and brought about their own certain destruction, at least exonerates them from the slanderous charge that they had betrayed their country of asylum. Marshal Pétain and Monsieur Laval were not refugees from Nazi oppression.

In England, the ultimate disaster which had overtaken and sealed the fate of the refugees in France was the signal for adopting France's refugee policy. But when all this is recognised and the charge of suspicion is withdrawn from the refugees (for lack of a shred of evidence to support it), there still remains the possibility of betrayal by men who, as one MP put it, 'have not discarded their native patriotism for ours'.

This, of course, is the crux of the matter. The 'native patriotism' of the anti-Nazi is the mainspring of his struggle against Hitler, who had degraded and enslaved the German people for long years before that process had been carried abroad. To identify the refugee with the régime of which he is the opponent or the victim is a piece of muddleheadedness so gross that it cannot be attributed to the British government, as the government spokesman in the House of Lords, the Duke of Devonshire, made clear:

> These refugees have obviously suffered ... at the hands of their own government ... but nevertheless some of them must retain some attachment to their own country ... It is a mistake to think it is a perfectly simple matter and that all people who are refugees in this country from Nazi oppression are necessarily one hundred per cent with us in their desire to see the *overthrow of the German nation.*[13] (our italics)

No, the political refugees who have sacrificed everything during the best years of their lives that the German people may triumph over Hitler are not at one with the Duke of Devonshire.

With regard to some of the racial refugees, the Duke was on safer ground, though only for the purpose of reversing the internment policy. Thousands of Jews, discouraged beyond all hope by the treatment they had received in Germany, escaped from that country with the sole desire of emigrating permanently. They had been rejected as citizens of their own country by its present rulers and had played no part in the political struggle to change those rulers. The unspeakable horrors which overtook them served to make them hate the very name of Germany. These refugees may desire to see the overthrow of the German nation insofar as they, too, make the false identification of Hitler with Germany and, if the Duke's test were valid, should have been liberated at once. Or does the government suppose that its treatment of these Jews has caused them to hate England also? It can make so little difference to the Jew whether his gaolers speak well or ill of freedom if he is still the prisoner.

For those who do not identify a people with its government, no such hatred of England was possible, even after the introduction of wholesale internment.

For the second time, the refugee organisations found their work violently diverted into fresh channels, this time back to rescue work; and now new sections of the British public, not hitherto associated with refugee aid, took up the question of the rights and liberties of refugees. Not since Munich had the correspondence columns of the press, both national and local, shown such preoccupation with the fate of Hitler's victims. One of the most interesting aspects of this tremendous public protest was the way in which parsons, teachers, rural councillors and correspondents from every walk of life, who had taken the trouble to sit down and address their local papers, insisted upon the necessity of treating this question of the refugees as an index of war aims. It was in the main the attack on democratic principles which roused the public.

Meanwhile, the refugee organisations, as in the early days, were besieged by thousands of desperate applicants. Their task this time was even more delicate: the refugees were to be rescued from the British government which subsidised the organisations. The pleading, wrangling, haggling machinery was set into motion again. But for the first many weeks even the information that the refugee organisations could give the desperate relatives of the interned was hopelessly inadequate. Later, and as a result of the deportation scandal, an official Information Bureau was established at St Stephen's House, Westminster, by the Home Office. This might have drawn off the torrent of enquiries coming to the refugee organisations, but did not do so because the officials knew rather little, and the refugees went pouring back to their old friends. A Central Department for Interned Refugees was set up jointly by the refugee committees and shortly developed into an instrument for the practical alleviation of internment camp conditions.

The more important refugee organisations, themselves supported by government money, were not free to allocate their funds as they pleased; pocket money and gifts to the internees had to be provided by public goodwill. The second appeal period for refugees opened, but this time no public appeals were necessary: the small contributions poured in a continuous stream into the internment camps, and the refugees knew that, after all, they were befriended by the British people.

3

In June 1940 Canada volunteered to take 6,000 to 7,000 prisoners of war and dangerous internees from the United Kingdom for safe keeping and Australia volunteered to take 10,000.

The categories to be sent were, in order of priority, prisoners of war, German merchant seamen who had been captured and ranked as civilian internees, and enemy aliens in category 'A' who had been interned for security purposes. These represented the 'dangerous classes', but the British government was fully apprised of the fact that only 3,000 to 4,000 of these people existed at that time and therefore a Committee of the Cabinet presided over by Mr Neville Chamberlain gave instructions that the balance was to be made up of 'B' and 'C' category refugees.

On 30 June, the *Arandora Star*, a vessel of 15,501 tons built in 1926 and reconditioned in 1929 to carry 360 passengers and a full crew, set sail for Canada with some 1,700 persons on board: 473 German and Austrian internees, of whom 123 were merchant seamen, 717 Italian internees, some 200 British troops to guard them (though none was a prisoner of war) and a crew of about 300.

This prison-ship, carrying two-and-a-half times as many people as it was designed for, in conditions reminiscent of convict transportations and slave-cargoes of the seventeenth century, was attacked and sunk by a U-boat off the west coast of Ireland at 6 a.m. on 2 July 1940.

One hundred and forty-three Germans and Austrians and 470 Italians lost their lives, but the total number of casualties, which included the captain and other ship's officers, members of the crew and British troops, was not revealed. Two further Germans and two Italians later died on board one of the rescue ships.

So much for the facts.

On 5 July the *Manchester Guardian* announced that many of the Italians had been men over 60 and that the German and Austrian internees had included young anti-Nazi refugees in category 'C', whose deportation had been kept secret from their families and from the official refugee organisations responsible for them.

On 7 July an official denial was issued stating that there was no truth whatever in the allegations that there had been category 'C' or any aliens classed as 'friendly' on board the *Arandora Star*.

On 9 July this point was further emphasised in the House of Commons by the Minister of Shipping (Mr Cross) who, in answer to uneasy questions, stated categorically that all the Germans on board had been Nazi sympathisers, none of whom had come to this country as a refugee. The Secretary of State for War had informed him of this and, further, none had category 'B' or 'C' or could be considered friendly aliens. Lists of the missing had been given, he said, to the Protecting Powers that the next-of-kin might be informed. The shipowners had taken steps to inform the next-of-kin of the members of the crew who had been lost. Although the accommodation in the vessel was known to be inadequate for the numbers it was carrying at the time, the Minister stated that lifeboats and rafts had been more than sufficient for those on board.

On 10 July during the debate on refugees in the House of Commons, Mr Peake, on behalf of the Home Office, quoted, with evident satisfaction, the Minister of Shipping's statement regarding the character of the internees on board the *Arandora Star* but, confronted by the names of two well-known German Trade Union leaders who went down with the ship and by the fact that 21 Austrian Socialists who had been on board had arrived back in this country and communicated with their friends, evaded the issue by asking honourable Members to consider the difficulties of arriving at the names of the missing and kindly explained the procedure involved. At this point a welcome distraction was afforded by Mr Logan, Member for Liverpool, Scotland Division (who gracefully helped out the government at various sticky points in the debate), under cover of which the Under-Secretary was able to launch into an exposition of the general policy governing the transportation of refugees.

Nevertheless, the fact that they were now called 'refugees' (when the Minister of Shipping had stated in so many words that 'none came to this country as refugees'); the fact that they were admitted to include single men in category 'B' when it had been said that: 'None had category "B" or "C" certificates'; the fact that 'where we have had to make up the number we have selected single men under the age of 50 and in preference with those who expressed a wish to go' (even though 'the Germans on board were Nazi sympathisers') – all this revealed a certain lack of inter-departmental co-ordination and it was a pity that the Home Office spokesman should have quoted in full Mr Cross's statement of the previous day and then proceeded to contradict it in every particular.

As early as 4 July the Home Office and the War Office had unofficially confirmed that both Nazis and anti-Nazis had been on board the *Arandora Star* while distracted relatives, enquiring whether their menfolk were interned in this country, interned in Canada or drowned, were directed by the Home Office – the interning authority – to the War Office, at that time in charge of internment camps, and thence to the Admiralty, who directed them back to the War Office, where it was hopefully suggested that lists of survivors from the *Arandora Star* would shortly be published by the Ministry of Information.

In view of the inability of the Ministry of Shipping and the Home Office to make out a consistent case and stick to it, the number of government departments now seen to be involved boded little good for those seeking reliable information.

On 17 July Mr Eden, Secretary of State for War, as a latecomer with apparently no one to tell him what had transpired in the first act, told the House of Commons that the interned enemy aliens on board the *Arandora Star* were Italian fascists and category 'A' Germans, none of whom was a refugee. This was particularly unfortunate in view of the fact that the friends of missing and surviving refugees were now in possession of a great deal of contrary evidence and had supplied it to Members of Parliament. In stating further that there had been no prisoners of war on board the vessel, Mr Eden gave the *coup de grâce* to the Home Office case, which had been based precisely on a general policy of deporting prisoners of war. (It is referred to as the Home Office case, since the Home Office spokesman was obliged to deputise for the author of the deportation policy, Mr Chamberlain, who absented himself from the House and the existence of whose Committee was only elicited under considerable pressure in the course of the debate. It is here assumed that as between this Committee and the Home Office there was no discrepancy of views.)

By 19 July the War Office had become touchy and was refusing to say whether refugees had or had not been on board the torpedoed ship.

On 23 July – three weeks after the sinking – an intrepid voice in the House of Commons enquired whether the Germans and Austrians in the *Arandora Star* had all been Nazi sympathisers. Mr. Eden replied that instructions had been issued for immediate enquiries to be made.

On 6 August it was revealed to the House of Lords how the statement that there had been only category 'A' refugees on board was to be interpreted:

> I have been into that question of transhipment, and it is a fact that there were no category C people on board [the *Arandora Star*]. Of the 473 Germans and Austrians on board, it has been verified that all these had been individually ordered to be interned on grounds of national security. Accordingly, they came within category A.[14]

On 22 August Mr Attlee, the Lord Privy Seal, informed a Member that his 'Noble Friend Lord Snell has been asked to undertake an inquiry into the selection of aliens to be sent overseas in the *Arandora Star*'.[15]

In December an inconclusive summary of Lord Snell's report[16] was presented by Mr Attlee to the House. The outstanding fact in this summary is that the deportees are referred to throughout as Germans, Austrians and Italians, or simply as enemy aliens, and nowhere is the word 'refugee' used. Lord Snell did not consider that the errors by which 26 of the 717 Italians were not those intended for deportation and whose names had been supplied to camp commandants was a cause for serious criticism. He stated that all the Germans and Austrians 'could properly be regarded as coming within category "A"'.

As we have the eye-witness accounts of friends among the interned refugees who thought they were being shipped to the Isle of Man, wished to remain together, and therefore volunteered for and were accepted by the deportation authorities in place of others, while some refugees who did not want to go paid substitutes to take their place, Lord Snell's certainty about the identity of passengers on the *Arandora Star* must rest mainly on the fact that the individuals concerned are at the bottom of the sea.

Now this sample of administrative 'inefficiency' demonstrates that, if and when, for reasons of State, the government decides upon a course of action which is detestable to the majority of decent and responsible human beings, it has in readiness the most highly perfected machinery of 'muddle' and 'incompetence', so constructed that even an awkward accident (such as a torpedoed vessel) cannot do more than reveal without dislocating the well-oiled works.

Further revelations were provided by the incidents of the MS *Ettrick* and the SS *Dunera*. The following description of conditions on the MS *Ettrick* has been compiled from reports by two of the passengers:

> The M.S. *Ettrick* left Liverpool on 3rd July 1940 with 1,300 internees on board, of whom over 1,200 were refugees.
>
> Twelve hundred and eighty-four people were herded together in the bows of the ship in a three-tiered space with a shaft in the centre. The three tiers were connected by companion ways – the top tier was at about sea level. Most of the space available for these 1,284 people was taken up by the dining tables, benches, the shaft and the companion ways. At the top level, which was naturally a larger space than the bottom tier in the hold of the ship, over 500 people lived and slept for twelve days and nights. Another 500 prisoners were put in the Sergeants' Mess. There were a few ratings on board, but most of the guards were soldiers. There were some German military prisoners of war, kept apart from the internees and evidently in quite decent conditions; they had cabins to sleep in and seemed to be allowed on a certain part of the deck at any time of day.

In the event of an emergency the only way out for the internees on the lower tiers would have been the companion way and from there to the lower deck, but at the top of the companion way there was a barbed wire barrier which left a space of some 4ft. for passage during the day, but was entirely closed and under military guard during the night. To reach the upper deck and the lifeboats the prisoners would have had to get through another barbed wire barrier and two further companion ways which were always heavily guarded while the doors at the top of the companion ways were kept locked.

Amongst the first news the internees had on embarking was the sinking of the *Arandora Star*. Most of them were no longer capable of standing up, so they sat or lay about wherever there was available space. The only supply of air came through the ventilating pipes which ran through the body of the ship. Late in the evening the ship sailed and later still the internees had their first meal of the day.

Not enough hammocks and blankets were issued to the internees. People slept on the dining tables, on the benches, on the floor, on the companion way, literally on top of each other.

For two days they were not allowed to emerge, for they were not to see any part of the Scottish or Irish coast, so they stayed below decks for two days and two nights. After that, congestion was relieved during the day-time by two-hourly shifts of half the complement on deck. There were two inadequate meals a day, one at 8 a.m. and one at 6 p.m.

Many people were sea-sick almost the whole time, and a few buckets were allotted to them, and put down among the people who had to lie on the floor at night. During the second night a sudden epidemic of diarrhoea broke out. The gangway leading to the lavatories was closed by barbed wire, and as the guards refused to open them even in an emergency, people had to relieve themselves wherever they stood or happened to be. This situation was repeated during the following night, and the prisoners were finally granted another few buckets, for which there was hardly any room left on the floors where people were lying. A number of internees appeared to be going mad, they had cramp, yelled in despair, struggled to break through the barbed wire, while others went on vomiting from the hammocks, from the tables and benches, or tried to reach a bucket, treading on other people's faces and hands. There were several attempts at suicide.

Even on deck the internees were only granted a limited space, on one side of the ship, its boundaries heavily guarded.

One morning, when one shift of 300 odd people was taken on deck and kept to one side to wait until the previous shift had gone below, a sergeant, while trying to push people back, suddenly pulled out a heavy rubber truncheon and beat ten or fifteen people about the head. This performance took place under the eyes of the German prisoners of war, who stood on the other side of the partition and no doubt enjoyed this re-enactment of concentration camp scenes. The sergeant also tried to grab a bayonet from one of the sentries, but the sentry refused to let go (and was later charged by the sergeant for disobeying orders). There was an uproar among the crowd of refugees.

The officer commanding the transport refused to see representatives of the internees throughout the voyage. His expressions, such as 'you lousy lot', 'scum of the earth', showed that he was well aware that the internees were refugees. One of the internees, who was a qualified medical man, wrote a letter to the officer in command to draw his attention to the appalling conditions in which the refugees were living, while the passenger quarters were practically empty. The result of this letter was that the doctor who had written it was put in a cell for twenty-four hours. The officer, referring to the doctor's claim to be an anti-Nazi refugee, shouted at him: 'Who are you? You're nobody. You're one of those low birds nesting everywhere.' On the day the ship docked in Canada, the Colonel, being unable to cope with the disembarkation, lost his head and shouted at everyone. He kicked and beat one of the internees, a small Jewish boy, shouting: 'Get back, you lousy lot.' Later he ordered the sentries to use their bayonets against the refugees (which they did not do).

During the whole of the voyage those internees who were not sick all the time worked every day and all day long trying to keep their quarters clean and to establish some sort of organisation in these chaotic conditions.

Internees going up to the passenger deck were told to take lifebelts with them, but it was not until the fifth day out that lifebelts were issued. There was not a single boat drill and, as has already been said, the internees were allowed on only a very small part of the passenger deck, and therefore did not have access to most of the lifeboats.

When handing in their luggage at one English camp before their departure, the internees had been told that they would not be able to get at their belongings until they had embarked. As they were to go on board on the same day as they left the camp, many did not trouble to carry soap, a towel, toothbrush etc. to Liverpool. On arriving at the ship, however, they were informed that they would not be allowed to take anything from their bags or cases until they had reached their destination. For the same reason they had to wear the same clothes for twelve days and nights.

The refugees transported in the MS *Ettrick* in these conditions came from the Isle of Man camps and Huyton. The refugees at Central Camp Douglas had been informed during the last week of June that all unmarried men between twenty and thirty would soon be leaving the camp. The categories of those who were to leave were given out as Orthodox Jews, Liberal Jews, Catholics and Protestants. On 2nd July, half an hour before leaving, this group was joined by about twenty-five older men who had been selected individually by the camp commandant and classified as 'trouble-makers'. This group included some prominent anti-Nazis. The group from Huyton camp had only been informed the day before their departure that they would be 'transferred'. As they had been told shortly before that they would all be transferred sooner or later to the Isle of Man, they assumed that this was their destination. The group was supposed to consist of unmarried people aged 20 to 35 years. Many married men, however, found their names on the list and decided to go, hoping to be reunited later with their wives on the Isle of Man. A number of men up to the age of fifty as well as boys of sixteen and seventeen were to leave as well. Several people tried to get out of it, simply did not hand in their luggage and bribed friends to go in their place. Similarly a group of friends agreed to leave together, not wishing to be separated. There was apparently no time to draw up a list of those who actually did leave, the main thing was to muster the right number of people embarking. Everybody was searched, matches and lighters were confiscated. No hand baggage was allowed. A professional musician had to negotiate for an hour with the officer in charge for a permit to take his violin with him.

Even after the ship left no one was told the destination. The refugees from Huyton had thought they were going to the Isle of Man. Some refugees from the Isle of Man had suspected that they were being sent to Huyton. When the two groups met on board ship it became clear beyond doubt that they were being shipped overseas.

After their arrival in the Canadian camp all the refugees' belongings were taken away by NCOs and privates. They were told that everything would be returned the next morning. However, when two days later the luggage and confiscated goods were returned, it was discovered that money and such things as watches, pens, lighters etc. had disappeared. While the luggage was laid out for examination and collection, the thieving continued. Several typewriters were stolen under the eyes of their owners and various other objects were 'confiscated' from suitcases. An investigation amongst the refugees revealed that money and articles to the value of £1,200 were missing.

On 25 March 1941, a question was asked in the House of Commons about conditions on board the MS *Ettrick* and whether action was to be taken against those responsible for them. Captain Margesson, Secretary of State for War, replied:

> The majority of the complaints about the conditions on board relate to accommodation and to the discomfort which arose as a result of overcrowding. As it was essential that the ship should be filled to capacity, the accommodation of passengers was necessarily restricted, and some discomfort was, I regret to say, inevitable. No complaint of general ill-treatment, brutality, or indiscipline on the part of the military escort, however, has been received, and although there may have been some evidence of unsympathetic treatment by individuals, I am satisfied that it is not of such a nature as to warrant trial by court-martial.[17]

A debate in the House of Commons on 25 February 1941 revealed that conditions on board the SS *Dunera*, carrying 2,400 internees to Australia, had been even worse than those on the MS *Ettrick*. The refugees, mostly Jews with 'C' certificates, had been transported in a ship built to carry only half that number. They had been robbed by the soldiers in charge and kept battened down, being allowed on deck only on certain occasions.

Colonel Wedgwood, who raised the matter, stated that he had taken the relevant correspondence to the Secretary of State for the Dominions, who had advised him to take it up with the Home Office. Thence it went to the War Office. Colonel Wedgwood urged that a Court of Inquiry be set up without delay and that the matter should be given publicity. In his reply Mr Richard Law, Financial Secretary to the War Office, stated:

> My right hon. Friend devoted the earlier part of his remarks to an appeal for the fullest possible publicity to be given to any inquiry there might be on the case of the *Dunera*. I wish I could persuade him that that is not necessarily the right attitude to follow in a case of this kind … If the allegations are proved to be well-founded, I can foresee certain definite disadvantages in washing our dirty linen in public in a world which contains enemies as well as friends …
>
> If we establish a Court of Inquiry it will be held in secret and it may be months before it completes its inquiry. In fact, it may prove impossible to complete it until the end of the war.[18]

In both cases the responsible authorities were favoured by a time lag which took the edge off the indignation felt by the public at these outrages. The sufferings of the refugees were a thing of the past by the time the facts became known and when the promised Court of Inquiry in the case of the *Dunera* has finished its investigation (after the war) it may be assumed that the public protest will have spent itself. In the case of the *Arandora Star*, as with internment camp conditions, the swiftness of the revelations, fully and widely publicised in the press and Parliament, forced the authorities to improve matters. The forced deportations in these conditions of unspeakable horror ceased in August 1940 and the camps, taken out of War Office hands at the same time, underwent certain salutary changes.

The object of the transportations, as explained in the House of Lords, was

> ... both to husband our resources of food and get rid of useless mouths and so forth, and to release the services of as many camp guards as possible...[19]

at a time when the risk of invasion was imminent. Mr Attlee told the House of Commons on 13 August that, because of the large numbers of aliens concentrated in a comparatively small number of camps, it was decided to send 9,420 Germans, Austrians and Italians to Canada and Australia.

It is a striking fact that these two official statements fail to explain why the refugees so deported were put into internment camps when they reached Canada and Australia, where the risk of invasion was not imminent.

Of course, saving the food of 9,420 persons in a population of 48 million in a time of emergency may be a good thing. But it so happens that this explanation for the transhipment of aliens followed, by scarcely two weeks, the government's decision to curtail and possibly suspend altogether its scheme for the evacuation of children to safety overseas.

When we know that in the 1914–18 war all enemy alien internees (amongst whom were no refugees) were employed in some form or other as the demand for labour increased, we may ask why internees in this war should have been designated 'useless mouths' while tens of thousands of children, who cannot do useful work, who require the services of thousands of adults, and who are the first and worst sufferers from any food deficiencies, were prevented from going abroad, although the British public – to judge from the numbers of registrations by parents under the scheme – wanted them to go.

Many persons in authority have questioned the common sense of the conditions under which the deported aliens were held – in a comparatively small number of camps and under armed guard. Yet to release the refugees – and thereby their guards – and give them honest work to do was for some reason an unthinkable alternative.

One has only to consider the atrocious suffering caused to individuals by the deportation policy to realise immediately that other reasons than the very practical ones advanced must have motivated it. Not a single government spokesman has offered excuses – as in the case of the 'muddles' in carrying out the internment policy – for the tragedies attendant upon the transhipments. But for the sinking of the *Arandora Star*, neither the public nor the relatives of the refugees on board might have heard of her ill-fated cargo; no public discussion of the general policy might have taken place for months. Even while MPs pressed the cases of separated families, transported youths, lost relatives, the government attempted to give no reasoned replies and very few reassuring ones.

The anxiety of those left behind could have been alleviated by so small a step as informing wives and mothers of the proposed transhipments and safe arrival overseas. While mothers waited for news which never came, wives of deported aliens were informed after some lapse of time that they could rejoin their husbands overseas. They gave up their homes and their jobs if they had any, and flocked to London from all over the country. There they learnt that the arrangements had been cancelled at the eleventh hour and there they remained, destitute and bewildered, without help or hope.

In picturing their plight it must be remembered that the wife of an interned man could not claim Public Assistance or Unemployment Benefit, since the government had rendered her husband ineligible for employment by interning him. But both the wives who were themselves interned and those left outside, whatever material ills they suffered, were chiefly broken by the cruelty of the separation, which was of a truly terrible poignancy for those who had shared for years the strains and dangers of their men both in exile and before it. For the right to be beside them, at once their duty and their happiness, they had sacrificed every other duty and every other happiness, abandoned their homes, left all associations dear to them. They now declared that they would not have minded the hardships, the perils of transportation, the discomforts and worse of camp life to retain this one remaining right. The bitterness of that wrenching apart in exile, and the finality of the parting which the unheralded deportations spelt, condemned them to an indescribably cold and lonely misery.[20]

Granted that the deportations were undertaken with a haste which did not allow for notifying relatives, a chance for the men to collect their belongings or to repossess themselves of identity papers and the like, there is still no reason why the central refugee organisations should not have been informed of the intention to deport, so that they could have arranged for some equivalent form of welfare to be set up in the overseas countries. Obeying government edicts to the letter, these bodies could in no way have interfered with the official plan but, by calling upon the organised aid of such humane and interested parties, some alleviation of the worst sufferings, injustices and confusions might have been effected on the arrival of the internees, and some word of comfort might have been sent to their relatives in Britain. The secrecy of the deportations, shattered by the sinking of the *Arandora Star*, denied the exiles even so much kindness: the central refugee committees did not know of their departure.

What of the governments of the reception Dominions?

Ottawa had volunteered in June 1940 to take prisoners of war and dangerous internees, but had no jurisdiction over those who were sent: they had accepted a purely contingent responsibility for supplying suitable prison quarters and military guards for 'dangerous prisoners', so there was very little they could do immediately. After two months of protest and memoranda from the interned refugees, the authorities showed their recognition that the majority of their prisoners sent from England were not Nazis at all but refugees from Nazi oppression. Thereafter, and within the limits of the regulations, conditions improved and the separation of the Nazis from the refugee groups began. Nevertheless the status of prisoner of war and the restrictions that implied were unaltered.

As for the Australian government, when it found that there were no prisoners of war and no category 'A' aliens among the arrivals, it refused to continue with the scheme and proposed as an alternative to take wives and children so that the families of those already transhipped might be reunited. This offer, however, was not found to be 'in the interests of the parties concerned' or 'practicable' by the British government.[21]

One factor which rendered the position of the refugees so serious was that, being deported as prisoners of war and dangerous civilian internees, they were treated in accordance with the International Convention for Prisoners of War (1929), which made them liable to exchange.

The reports of survivors from the *Arandora Star*, and passengers in the *Ettrick* and *Dunera*, no less than the ambiguous statements of official spokesmen, show that the transportations had been undertaken without the knowledge or consent of most of those to be transported. Some of the transhipped refugees were under consideration for release from internment. They were, in fact, being favourably considered by one government department while another spirited the applicants away and out of reach. Great issues must undoubtedly have been at stake beside which these sufferings and injustices had but small significance.

At this point it is important to step back and gain a clear perspective of the refugee population in this country in relation to internal politics. Whether the refugees individually are racial victims or political opponents of fascism, they represent a very definite anti-fascist democratic force by their very existence. Whether they are politically minded themselves or not, their absorption into British national life acts as an automatic brake on mindless anti-German chauvinism among the British population: even the least-informed public and one most accessible to chauvinist propaganda is readily influenced by actual contact with a decent German refugee.

The Nazi advance in Europe in the spring of 1940 produced a critical situation at home which forced a change of government. The new government set about rallying British morale and mobilising practical and psychological support for the war, but it was not considered desirable to encourage the free circulation of refugees from fascism among the British people and to allow their very presence to contradict official propaganda with its new emphasis on the German, rather than the fascist, nature of the enemy.

Moreover, it had long been foreseen, as the Order in Council of 17 November 1939 indicates, that the existence in their midst of tens of thousands of foreigners living on public or charitable funds in idleness, however radically reduced that standard of living, would prove a focus of discontent for the British people. The removal of the refugees was timed to coincide with such domestic causes for discontent as abnormally prolonged working hours, lowered purchasing power and intensified military call-up.

The internment policy was officially announced as a temporary measure, and the equipment of the camps provides evidence that, although the policy was not put into force overnight, as has been suggested, it was planned in haste. That there would be an outcry against it and perhaps a very dangerous outcry, and that the applause of a free press would not be hearty or long, was recognised from the start in government circles. At the same time, however, the government had not the slightest intention of reversing its policy and, in order to ensure its effectiveness in all circumstances, deportations were ordered.

The majority of the deportees were young men between the ages of 16 and 35 whose continued internment was unjustifiable for manpower reasons. It was clear that the most telling campaign, and one that would rally the greatest public support, would be launched precisely on the grounds that valuable labour power was being wasted. Therefore the young male refugees were removed and Members of Parliament could make themselves hoarse in Westminster: the young men were safely in Canada and Australia. They, of course, were in the category of refugees most likely to be absorbed into industry and to merge with the main stream of British labour.

The deportees included the majority of the small number of responsible German, Austrian and Italian political refugees in this country. For them, oddly enough, there was no upper age limit. In this way the conscious anti-fascist forces amongst the refugees in Britain were deliberately weakened by the government's action.

Another and even more serious reason for the deportations, and the one which the refugees themselves recognised immediately, was that the invasion and capitulation of France had introduced the possibility of similar events in Britain. If such a contingency occurred, Britain and the Dominions would be at a great disadvantage for exchanging prisoners of war. The Germans had captured on the Western Front considerable numbers of Empire troops. The Dominions therefore had their own interest in holding German prisoners of war in custody.[22]

The deported refugees had been classified as 'Prisoners of War Class II Civilians'. They were not allowed to write letters on any paper other than official forms with the imprint 'Prisoners of War Mail'. For one month the majority of them preferred not to communicate with their families at all as a protest against the classification and for fear of endangering the recipients. Communications to the refugees from their relatives had to be sent to the Director of Operations, Base Army Post Office, Ottawa, and in the case of refugees in Australia to the Prisoners of War Information Bureau, Melbourne. Sleeping huts were locked at night, and there was barbed wire on all windows. Machine-guns were trained on the camps and every refugee was issued with specially marked prisoner-of-war clothing and his photograph and fingerprints were taken.

Having had an eye to prisoners of war for possible exchange purposes, the reactions of the Canadian and Australian authorities when they found that anti-fascist refugees and 16-year-old Jewish boys figured very prominently in the transports were those of pure dismay.

As the first wave of alarm and despondency roused by the capitulation of France subsided, it became obvious that the storm over the internment policy would break and this doubtless accounts for the indecent haste and secrecy with which the deportations were rushed through.

4

The storm broke in the House of Commons on 10 July and raged for close on six hours.

> This is a question which affects our prestige as a nation, and we do not want to let it go out that our land is a land of oppression and not a land of the free …

said Miss Eleanor Rathbone,[23] that staunch and experienced champion of the refugees.

I believe that in creating an atmosphere in England that all Germans are suspect, Hitler has again succeeded in winning a propaganda victory over this country. I am certain that the one thing Hitler wants to establish as far as national consciousness in this war is concerned, is that it is a war of all Germans against the British. If he can establish that, he gets unity in his own country …

said Mr Wilfrid Roberts.[24]

When the war broke out, we were not, according to the then Prime Minister, fighting the German people. We were fighting Hitlerism … Refugees came to this country, and many people used their influence to bring them here. Money was subscribed in large quantities in order to support and help them … It was advertised far and wide as being a unique effort in the treatment of refugees.

That vision has now been shattered and, as we know, the utmost use is being made in Germany of this fact, with appropriate headlines from the English Press, with the object of showing that the enemies of Hitler in Germany are now the enemies of England. They ask, 'Where are the much-vaunted cultural virtues of Democracy?' That is what they are saying in Germany, and are beginning to say in America. They are saying that there is now no difference between the enemies of Nazism and of Democracy. That may seem to some people a matter of small consequence, but it is, in reality, of the utmost consequence, because the regeneration of Europe depends upon people who have still, in Germany and in other countries, democratic and reasonable sentiments. These beliefs are being shattered by the treatment of refugees in the last few weeks …

said another Member, Mr Graham White,[25] and:

We are only playing Hitler's game if we do not make amends to these people and deal summarily and promptly with the problem which now confronts us …

said Lord Davies in the Upper House in August;[26] and these spokesmen carried the full weight of public opinion behind them.

The Home Office affected to believe that it was faced by a capricious turn in public feeling and that it was pulled, now this way and now that, in its tireless efforts to please.[27] But search as one may through the press and parliamentary reports of this period, there is only one inconsistency to be found: the newspapers which applauded and upheld the Home Secretary's decision of 11 May – communicated to them in the circumstances we know and doubtless presented as a strictly limited category of temporary internments – were very soon protesting vigorously at the all-embracing nature of the policy, the repellent character of its application and the conditions of the internment camps. As for the Members of Parliament, not one of those who now objected to the internments had spoken a word in favour of such action in May.[28]

The weakness of the government's case can best be judged by the reply of Sir Edward Grigg, speaking for the War Office, in answer to the debate, his Department being then in charge of the internment camps and responsible for their conditions. It was not the disingenuousness of this reply – although a phrase suggesting that refugees in internment camps were in no greater danger from Nazi invaders than English children in schools can scarcely have been due to complete ignorance of the events in other European countries or of Article 19 of the Franco-German armistice – but its bluster which was so striking.

Despite the view, expressed from every part of the House, that here was an appalling situation which went to the very root of the values Britain was said to be fighting for, this responsible government representative brushed aside so trivial a consideration in these words:

> I have listened to the greater part of this Debate, and I am bound to say that I have never been more greatly struck by one of the great qualities of the House of Commons, and that is its power of detachment. There has been going on this afternoon, I suppose, one of the greatest air battles of the war. At this moment – I do not know whether it is so – bombers may be over a number of our towns ... In the approach of many Members of this House to this problem there was an atmosphere of unreality which to me was positively terrifying.
>
> I wonder how many Members have ever tried to put themselves in the place of the men who are actually responsible for the security of this country and are not concerned with merely making speeches ...
>
> This country has always been a great asylum to the distressed refugees from other countries, but it would be foolish not to recognise that, in the opinion of its own people, it is beginning to be a great asylum in another sense.[29]

So, with shabby quips of this kind, and an attempt to make Members feel that they were idle chatterboxes in raising a question of fundamental aims for which Members supposed the air-battles of the day were being fought, the War Office gave an insight into its fitness to deal with the refugee matters that had been entrusted to it.

Mr Peake, on behalf of the Home Office, dealt with the question seriously:

> ... I should like to pay my tribute to the behaviour of these refugees in that they have shown themselves worthy of the confidence which we have placed in them ... As far as category 'C' aliens are concerned against whom nothing is known, careful instructions have been given to the police as to the exceptions which they are to make, and I hope and believe that these instructions are being carefully followed ...
>
> In the first place, persons under 16 and over 70 are exempted. The invalids and the infirm are exempted, and the police have special instructions that a person should be regarded as exempted if he can produce medical evidence which satisfies the police that he needs continuous medical attention ... The instructions include categories of persons who are engaged as key workers in industries performing work of national importance, and categories of persons granted permits to work by the Aliens War Services Department. There are doctors of medicine and dentists who have been given permission by the Secretary of State to practise in this country. There are persons whose emigration from this country has been arranged ... There are members who either are in, or have been in, the Auxiliary Military Pioneer Corps. There are persons holding key positions in refugee organisations, and in certain circumstances persons who employ British labour where British labour will be thrown out of employment if their employers, the aliens, are interned. Then there are persons who have a son or sons, serving in the Navy, Army or Air Force, and persons engaged in agriculture, food growing or forestry.[30]

Thus for the first time it became known that a very large number of refugees, including those upon whom the hardships of the camps fell most severely, had been interned entirely by mistake. This, however, was not calculated to reassure the House, since whether the inhumanity was due to planning or bungling it could not counteract the evil impression given to all democrats here and abroad, nor yet undo the sufferings sustained by the refugees.

The upshot of this debate was that on 23 July, Sir John Anderson, the then Home Secretary, announced in the House of Commons that responsibility for the camps would now pass from the War Office to his own Department, that categories of persons eligible for release from internment were to be published forthwith and that it had been decided to appoint an Advisory Committee to assist him in dealing with the problem of control of enemy aliens, and an Advisory Council to be attached to the Refugee Department of the Foreign Office.

The terms of reference of these two advisory bodies were made known shortly afterwards. The tasks of the Advisory Committee, under the Chairmanship of the Hon. Mr Justice Asquith, were:

1) to keep under review the application of the principles laid down in regard to the internment of enemy aliens and to make to the Home Secretary such suggestions and recommendations thereon as they think fit;

2) to advise the Home Secretary on such proposals for modifying the internment policy as he may refer to them from time to time;

3) to examine, and make recommendations upon, such individual cases as may be referred to them from time to time by the Home Secretary.

The functions of the Advisory Council, with Lord Lytton as its Chairman, were:

a) to suggest measures for maintaining the morale of aliens in this country so as to bind them more closely to our common cause;

b) to review and if necessary to suggest measures for the co-ordination, to the end described in a) above, of the work of the various refugee committees and other voluntary organisations concerned with aliens in this country;

c) to maintain contact with the various government Departments having responsibilities in connection with refugees and other classes of aliens and with foreign governments or National Committees established in this country;

d) to advise and assist the Home Office in the arrangements made for the welfare of enemy aliens in internment camps;

e) to study, and make recommendations upon, the problem of finding occupations for enemy aliens in internment camps.

It is no reflection upon the Council nor yet upon the Committee that these bodies were set up at a time, and after experiences, which had savagely challenged the 'common cause' to which the refugees were to be more closely bound, and when the co-ordination of refugee work had been rendered practically impossible by the lack of co-ordination of government departments dealing with refugee matters, compared with which the refugee committees, though largely run and staffed by amateurs, were a model of efficiency. It is not suggested that this eleventh-hour move, forced upon the government by public indignation, was nothing but a sop, for there is no question but that some of the people now asked to use their knowledge and ability would, in truth, humanise all dealings with the refugees; but it is to be noted that this work was intended to serve the purpose of applying the principles laid down in government policy and not to change it.

The first 18 categories of persons eligible for release from internment, as published in a White Paper on 31 July,[31] were found to include all those specified by Mr Peake, whom the government had interned by mistake, and six other categories.[32]

The White Paper referred only to category 'C' Germans and Austrians, and the test of whether they fell within the given categories was not related to their political reliability – in itself not grounds for release. This point and the complete inadequacy of the move led to another stormy session in the House of Commons. Major Cazalet said:

> ... I regret to say that the more I and some of my friends studied that White Paper the less satisfactory it appeared to be. It does not matter whether there are 18 or 80 categories in a White Paper if those categories do not apply to the people who are interned.[33]

A further White Paper was promised during this debate and published a few days later.[34] It reduced the age of eligibility for release from 70 to 65 years (category 1) and added a new category (19):

> Any person as to whom a Tribunal, appointed by the Secretary of State for the purpose, reports that enough is known of his history to show

> that by his writings or speeches or political or official activities he has consistently, over a period of years, taken a public and prominent part in opposition to the Nazi system and is actively friendly towards the Allied Cause.

Further categories, it was stated, would be added as a result of the review which the Advisory Committee had been asked to undertake, and the cases of category 'B' applicants who had not had their cases reviewed by the second tribunals (Regional Advisory Committees), but who were otherwise eligible under the White Paper, would be referred to a special tribunal.

In considering these two White Papers, it is to be noted that the July Paper was entitled 'German and Austrian Civilian Internees' and the August one 'Civilian Internees of Enemy Nationality', neither of which designation can be said to apply to the refugees who had been deprived of their German or Austrian nationality, who were in many cases 'stateless' and in no case enjoyed, 'in law or in fact, the protection of the German government'.[35] Furthermore, the term 'civilian internees' is commonly understood and in official speeches is generally intended to refer to German, Austrian and Italian subjects, living in this country on the declaration of war against their governments, who owe allegiance to these belligerent governments, are interned for that reason, and whose interests are looked after by a Protecting Power. Possibly the term, inept as it is to describe refugees, was meant to ensure that its usual connotation should not be overlooked for the purposes of release. Nor should it be forgotten that there were 13,000 non-refugee Germans and Austrians in category 'C'.

The very titles, therefore, under which the releases of refugees were to be considered nullified the provisions of the Geneva Convention. Scarcely a month before the military authorities had presented their case for internment to the Home Secretary, instructions had been issued to the police that 'stateless' persons of German or Austrian origin should, for all practical purposes, be regarded as Germans. (What the practical purpose of the police was in this matter was not then revealed; but the instructions to the police of 15 April shed an interesting light on the 'suddenness' of Sir John Anderson's conversion on 11 May.)

Certainly the registration of 'stateless' refugees as Germans and the designation of all German and Austrian refugees as enemy aliens simplified the administration of the internment policy and, though it was legalistically absurd to lump under the same head the German Nazi, whether for arrest or release, with the persecuted Jew or political exile, it was consistent with the degrading practice of herding the two elements together in the physical proximity of overcrowded internment camps.

> It [the internment policy] is based upon the principle that what matters is whether a person is a German or not, whereas what really matters is whether he is a Nazi or not. That ought to be the real test ...

said Lord Cecil in the House of Lords,[36] and the strongest criticism was aroused because the White Papers failed to take this fundamental fact into account.

The special category designated in the second White Paper, intended as a concession – the sole one – to political refugees as such, excluded Communists[37] and, of course, all those young men and women who had, at best, taken part in the youth and student activities of the anti-fascist movement but could lay claim to no 'writings or speeches or political or official activities' over a 'period of years'. It also involved a loyalty test by incorporating the phrase 'actively friendly towards the Allied cause'. A tribunal was to consider all the information available and advise the Home Secretary whether each applicant was eligible for release. This tribunal was to consist of 'a chairman of legal experience ... assisted by two or three people appointed because of their knowledge of the politics of Germany and Austria', and could call upon certain selected representatives of refugees for additional information and advice 'as and when it is thought fit'.[38]

While this category gave grudging and conditional recognition to the few prominent refugee socialists and liberals – MPs, Trade Union leaders, publicists and the like – whose standing and records should have rendered them immune to the indignities of internment in the first place, the heirs to their traditions, those who in the nature of things would carry on the struggle, were to spend their youth learning of the British cause of freedom from inside an internment camp.

In point of fact, the formulation devised for this special category automatically excluded the majority of the political refugees: the rank-and-file members of the German and Austrian opposition movements, the minor officials of Trade Unions, those whose work consisted of the dangerous and difficult day-to-day activities of organising resistance to Hitler in factories and offices, rather than in writing or delivering speeches, and was of necessity carried on clandestinely and was therefore not 'public and prominent'.[39]

Criticisms of the release categories, both in the Houses of Parliament and in the press, were also directed to the fact that they were based almost entirely on whether or not a man was useful.

> If these people on release can be of service to the national cause, we will let them out. That smells a little too much of Hitlerism for me. These men should be let out of the internment camps because they are innocent and not because they are useful. That is the test ...

said Mr Rhys Davies in the House of Commons.[40]

Perhaps the major objection to the categories for release was overlooked by most critics. This was that they embodied not only the Nazi principle of '*wirtschaftlich wertvoller Jude*' ('economically valuable Jew'), but also the Gestapo principle of releasing a man from internment on condition that he undertakes to work for the government which interned him.[41]

The danger of this is that it effectively takes from the individual his integrity – or his freedom (as in Germany). Insofar as the personal advantage of release was to be had by performing services dictated by the British government, the probity or otherwise of the refugee was put at a total discount. That the government itself was not blind to these implications is indicated by the statement of Sir John Anderson in the House of Commons on 22 August; when pointing out that the father of a Pioneer Corps recruit, even if the son died in action, was not entitled to release, he said:

> I do not want to be either hard or cynical, but a young man in internment who accepts an alternative offered to him of joining the Pioneer Corps is not in quite the same position as the ordinary volunteer.[42]

* * *

Stripped of all casuistry, the position was quite simply that, as far as the authorities were concerned, the refugees represented a danger which could not be publicly admitted; that bare tolerance had degenerated into fear and hostility; that these emotions had become so hysterical that the resultant action offended against public morals and that, in retreating from its worst excesses, the government revealed more plainly than ever before the nature of its mistrust of the refugees.

The series of 'release' White Papers was a testimony to official scepticism of the values trumpeted abroad: a man might be free in this Britain if he was too young or too old for the rigours of the concentration camps; he might be free if he could be put to this or that practical use; but that he should be free because he loved freedom and had suffered oppression was not so much as suggested.

> ... there will for a long time be many people – indeed, there may be some until the end of the war – who are in fact devoted to our cause but who nevertheless are not let out and left at liberty. To them we would say that the fact that they remain interned does not necessarily carry any imputation that His Majesty's government consider them as enemies ...

pronounced Lord Halifax in the House of Lords.[43]

By October, Mr Herbert Morrison had taken office as Home Secretary and releases were being granted at an average rate of some 450 a week, declining during the following three months to an average of 400.

A third White Paper, amending that of August, was published in October[44] and included three new categories, bringing the total to 22: eminent men of art, science, learning or letters; students who had been at a university or technical college at the time of their internment; and persons who satisfied a tribunal that they had lived in this country for at least 20 years, had severed their connections with the country of their nationality and by interests and associations were friendly towards Britain. Tribunals and Advisory Committees had been set up to deal with this category and also with German and Austrian refugees who had come from Nazi-invaded countries since the outbreak of hostilities and had thus not been through previous examination, as well as Germans and Austrians who had been placed in category 'B' by the first tribunals without further review by the Regional Advisory Committee before being interned.

Despite the additional categories, instructions were clearly given both to the public by the Minister and to the refugee by the internment camp officials that they were expected to qualify for release by demonstrating their loyalty to the Allied cause. Prominent anti-Nazis could do so by applying under category 19, showing that they had played a *public part* in opposition to the Nazi regime and were actively friendly to the Allied cause; the rest by enlisting in the Pioneer Corps, to be drafted for employment as and if required. For those too old or too ill for the Pioneer Corps, Mr Morrison promised a tribunal to whom they could prove 'that they are opposed to the Nazi or Fascist systems, that they are positively friendly towards the Allied cause, and that they will remain steadfast towards that cause in all circumstances',[45] which became category 23.

An important variation of his predecessor's policy introduced by Mr Morrison was his refusal to recognise any distinction between dangerous Nazis held as such and refugees who had not demonstrated their loyalty to the Allied cause. This move was contrary to the agreed principle, accepted by the government under public pressure in Sir John Anderson's time and to a certain extent carried out, that Nazis and refugees should not be forced to share the same confinement.[46]

It will be seen that Mr Morrison's only real innovation was category 23, and the government's interpretation of the phrase 'that they are opposed to the Nazi or Fascist systems', can best be seen from the fact that Mr Peake explained to the House of Commons that 'many of these persons are persons with divided loyalty, and it is extremely difficult to ascertain what their true feelings are ... Some of these people say they are pro-Germans, but object most strongly to being labelled pro-Nazi.'[47]

At the same period the government's anxiety to make use of the aliens in September 1939[48] was seen to have undergone a radical change.

Mr Bevin had announced the setting up of an International Labour Branch at the beginning of August. The functions of this branch, he had explained, would be to obtain full knowledge of the persons available for employment and to seek suitable openings for them in industrial or other work. He would not, the Minister stated, have anything to do with people who were interned, the question of whose release was a matter for the Home Secretary. By the end of 1940, the policy of the International Labour Branch was 'to associate them [the aliens] to the fullest possible extent with our war effort'.[49] In accordance with Home Office policy, that association was primarily to be effected by absorbing people into industry who had first applied for and obtained release from internment to join the Pioneer Corps. The former system of 'supplementary registers', introduced with the Order in Council of November 1939, was superseded by a scheme of National Labour Exchanges, through which the foreign nationals in this country could be formed into an 'International Labour Force' quite distinct from British labour and organised in national trade unions of their own.

While the Poles and Czechs, having 'governments' recognised by the British authorities, were able to set up such Labour Exchanges (and to exert considerable pressure on their 'subjects'), the Germans and Austrians had still to rely largely upon the machinery of the now government-subsidised refugee organisations, and were constantly under the threat of internment. Thus, for example, under a Ministry of Aircraft Production scheme an interned refugee was told that he would be released to take up a particular job in a given factory. He was not entitled to leave that job and was to be re-interned at once if he did so.

In such a situation, it was plain that the 'national trade unions', with a large proportion of refugees amongst aliens in this country, would not be very powerful or independent organisations and the British trade union movement was faced with far more dangerous competition than if the foreigners had been drafted into industry through the ordinary channels and organised into the appropriate British unions. Standards of wages and fair conditions of work are hardly likely to be maintained by 'unions' composed of workers under the permanent threat of internment. For the same reason the move was calculated to make British workers feel hostile to their refugee fellows, and the artificial segregation so proposed – with distinguishing badges and other such features – to keep the two elements divided.

By 22 January 1941, 10,000 releases of Germans, Austrians and

Italians under the various categories, including several hundred deportees, had been authorised.[50] Another 10,000 men and women were still interned in the United Kingdom and 6,000 overseas. Of these, 1,724 had enlisted in the Pioneer Corps, 112 had been released as prominent anti-fascists (out of 200 applications), and only one release had been authorised under 'steadfastness'. As late as 13 February there were only 1,926 releases under these three categories, despite the fact that, for the mass of refugees who had now suffered over nine months of internment, they presented the sole prospect of release. The total number of releases authorised by that time was 11,113, almost half of whom had been released under categories 1 (persons under 16 or over 65 years of age) and 3 (the invalid or infirm). A study of these figures shows further that amongst the persons released under categories 1 and 3 were deportees from Canada and Australia; positive proof that persons under 16 and over 65, as well as invalid and infirm persons, had been shipped overseas in the conditions described.

The vast majority of the refugees were genuine victims and opponents of Hitler. Their credentials as such had been accepted by both the Home Office on immigration and the tribunals on examination. Their records gave evidence that they were people of integrity and courage. The small number of applications under categories 12, 19 and 23 therefore indicates quite plainly that the majority of refugees was reluctant to apply for and obtain release on conditions which amounted to an oath of allegiance to the Allied cause which the government had persistently and in all circumstances refused to define. In a debate on the refugees the Duke of Devonshire, government spokesman in the House of Lords, had implied that the aim was the overthrow of the German *nation*; broadcasts and publications like Sir Robert Vansittart's *Black Record*, condemning the whole German people, had not been repudiated by the government; the exile Polish government published Jew-baiting propaganda with impunity . And on all these matters, criticism by the refugees would constitute an interference in Britain's domestic politics, which for seven years they have been officially, repeatedly and peremptorily forbidden.

When they came to Britain the refugees had to give an undertaking not to participate in the politics of the country. That, of course, was during the period when 'so long as there was the slightest prospect of reaching any settlement with the German Government it would have been wrong to do anything to embitter relations between the two countries'.[51] Suddenly they were expected to play an active part in British politics if they did not want to remain behind barbed wire for the duration of the war; or they must join the Pioneer Corps, a unit of the British army, with no guarantee whether their service would finish with the end of the war or where they would be sent, and without any indication of what their status would be after the war.

These men who had certainly shown themselves more 'steadfast' than many of our upstart anti-Nazi politicians, these men who throughout years had risked their lives daily in the illegal struggle against Hitler in their own country – armed only with their integrity and courage, supported only by their convictions; they who had not submitted to Hitler and had spent their best years in concentration camps, kicked and beaten – were now written off as inimical and no better than Nazis if they did not readily fling themselves into the active prosecution of the unstated war aims of the British and Allied governments.

Although this period in refugee policy was marked by its steady flow of releases from internment and the cessation of transhipments overseas, the political attitude deteriorated and there was no longer any evidence whatsoever in official utterances that the refugees from Nazi oppression had any function or duty, any roots or future, any hopes or cares outside the British war effort.

NOTES

1. Sir John Anderson, House of Commons, 22 August 1940 (*Official Report*, Vol. 364, col. 1543).
2. Mr Peake, House of Commons, 10 July 1940 (*Official Report*, Vol. 362, col. 1237).
3. Colonel Wedgwood, House of Commons, 10 July 1940 (*Official Report*, Vol. 362, col. 1246).
4. By now this term will have become meaningless. At the time, it was applied to the campaign for not talking in public as the enemy might be anywhere and everywhere: 'Careless Talk Costs Lives' (footnote added in 1968).
5. House of Commons, 22 August 1940 (*Official Report*, Vol. 364, cols 1449–50).
6. For example the broadcast on 30 May 1940 by Sir Neville Bland, former British Minister in Holland.

7. If the Home Office and the Government were anxious to prevent public opinion being 'panicked', why did we not have the information long ago? What has the Government done to try to correct the impression created by the stories which have appeared in the Press? I feel that the Home Office and the Government were very willing to accept newspaper propaganda and a public atmosphere of nervousness, as an excuse for carrying out a policy which they thought would not be altogether popular with the whole country. (Mr Wilfrid Roberts, House of Commons, 10 July 1940 (*Official Report*, Vol. 362, cols 1264–5))
8. Sir John Hope Simpson in his *Survey* divides Italian political emigration into four periods: (1) October 1922–26: into this period falls the murder of Matteotti (1924) and the beginning of open persecution of Italian socialists and communists; (2) 1926–29: this period saw the main political emigration, since in autumn 1926 laws were passed which provided for the death penalty for political offences and the Special Tribunal of the Fascist Militia was established; (3) 1929–July 1936 when the political emigration was sporadic, and (4) since the beginning of the Spanish Civil War (July 1936) which was followed by a new wave of political persecution and emigration.
9. In my view, the most humane thing to do with those aliens at that time, and with public feeling what it was, was to put them into temporary internment. (Mr Peake, House of Commons, 10 July 1940 (*Official Report*, Vol. 362, col. 1238))
10. It is strange how men's mentality works. We remember the horror that sprang up in this country when Hitler put Jews, Socialists and Communists into concentration camps. We were horrified at that, but somehow or other we almost took it for granted when we did the same thing to the same people. (Mr Rhys Davies, House of Commons, 22 August 1940 (*Official Report*, Vol. 364, col. 1529))
11. In June 1940 there were in France 250,000 Italian, 125,000 Spanish, 50,000 German and Austrian, 40,000 Polish and 20,000 Czech, Slovak and Sudeten German anti-fascist refugees, excluding Poles who had immigrated to France for political reasons some years before the war.
12. Article 19 of the Franco-German Armistice:

    All German prisoners of war to be released. The French Government to hand over all German subjects indicated by the German Government who are in France or French oversea territory. (Summary of Articles of Armistice terms issued by the Ministry of Information, 23 June 1940)
13. The Duke of Devonshire, replying to the Debate on Internment, House of Lords, 15 August 1940 (*Official Report*, Vol. 117, cols 262–3).
14. The Duke of Devonshire, House of Lords, 6 August 1940 (*Official Report*, Vol. 117, cols 135–6).
15. House of Commons, 22 August 1940 (*Official Report*, Vol. 364, col. 1478).
16. Cmd. 6238, *Summary of the Arandora Star Inquiry*, 1940.
17. House of Commons, 25 March 1941 (*Official Report*, Vol. 370, col. 410).
18. House of Commons, 25 February 1941 (*Official Report*, Vol. 369, cols 486–7).
19. The Duke of Devonshire, House of Lords, 6 August 1940 (*Official Report*, Vol. 117, col. 137).

20. In the meantime he has been deported, and his wife, on going to ask about him this morning, was told, 'We cannot tell you where he is; there is no way in which you can get in touch with him; you will be informed if he is dead'. (Sir Richard Acland, House of Commons, 22 August 1940 (*Official Report*, Vol. 364, col. 1575))
21. On 6 February 1941 Mr Herbert Morrison stated in the House of Commons in reply to a question:

    I have now learned that the Australian authorities are willing, subject to certain conditions, that the wives and children in question should go to Australia. The present lack of shipping facilities, however, presents a serious obstacle to this course and other considerations have arisen since the question was first considered which have an important bearing on the matter; for instance, a considerable number of the internees in Australia are prospective emigrants to the United States ... I am very grateful to the Australian government for their offer but I have come to the conclusion that at all events at present it is not practicable, or in the interests of the parties concerned, to avail ourselves of this offer. (*Official Report*, Vol. 368, col. 1066)
22. Nobody knows the course of this war and what is going to happen to us all, but there is a genuine fear that if they are treated as prisoners of war, when the war is over they may be returned to their native lands and to the jaws of death. (Mr Rhys Davies, House of Commons, 22 August 1940 (*Official Report*, Vol. 364, col. 1531))
23. House of Commons, 10 July 1940 (*Official Report*, Vol. 362, col. 1220).
24. House of Commons, 10 July 1940 (*Official Report*, Vol. 362, col. 1265).
25. House of Commons, 10 July 1940 (*Official Report*, Vol. 362, cols 1232–3).
26. House of Lords, 15 August 1940 (*Official Report*, Vol. 117, col. 260).
27. At one time the feeling in the country and in this House was entirely in favour of these refugees. That feeling changed in the early days in May. Today it is swinging back in the other direction. (Mr Peake, House of Commons, 10 July 1940 (*Official Report*, Vol. 362, col. 1239))
28. Another question is that of the treatment of refugees during the last two or three months – a question which concerns every Member of this House. I think the House of Commons ought to dissociate itself clearly, emphatically and unambiguously from any responsibility for the work of whatever Department is responsible for the terrible mistakes made in connection with the refugees. (Sir Henry Morris-Jones, House of Commons, 21 August 1940 (*Official Report*, Vol. 364, col. 1346))
29. Sir Edward Grigg, House of Commons, 10 July 1940 (*Official Report*, Vol. 362, cols 1295–6, 1299).
30. House of Commons, 10 July 1940 (*Official Report*, Vol. 362, cols 1236, 1241–2).
31. Cmd. 6217, *German and Austrian Civilian Internees: Categories of Persons Eligible for Release from Internment and Procedure to be Followed in Applying for Release*, July 1940.
32. These were categories 2, 5, 8, 10, 16 and 18 covering persons who, at the time of their internment, were under 18 years of age and residing with British

families or in educational establishments; persons who had had official permission to remain in an Aliens Protected Area; scientists, research workers and persons of academic distinction for whom work of national importance in their special fields was available; doctors and dentists who had permits to study for British degrees; Ministers of Religion if holding a spiritual charge, except Ministers of a German Church; and cases of extreme hardship, for example where a parent, wife or child was dangerously ill.

33. House of Commons, 22 August 1940 (*Official Report*, Vol. 364, col. 1532).
34. Cmd. 6223, *Civilian Internees of Enemy Nationality: Categories of Persons Eligible for Release from Internment and Procedure to be Followed in Applying for Release*, August 1940.
35. The definition of a refugee given in the Geneva Convention Concerning Refugees, February 1938.
36. House of Lords, 5 September 1940 (*Official Report*, Vol. 117, col. 383).
37. Captain Graham asked the Home Secretary whether

    he can assure the House that, in releasing from British internment camps those who have been hostile to Fascism, he is not releasing those whose devotion to the cause of Communist world revolution is as great a menace to the peace and institutions of this realm as either Fascism or Nazidom? Sir J. Anderson: Yes, Sir. I can give the assurance asked for. (House of Commons, 22 August 1940 (*Official Report*, Vol. 364, cols 1434–5))

38. Sir John Anderson, House of Commons, 22 August 1940 (*Official Report*, Vol. 364, cols 1551–2).
39. Miss Rathbone: Will it cover people who are active in trade unions, say, who are strongly social-democratic? It rather sounds as if it covered very high-up people and not working-class people who are strong anti-Fascist. Sir J. Anderson: The wording has been carefully considered ... (House of Commons, 22 August 1940 (*Official Report*, Vol. 364, col. 1551))
40. On 22 August 1940 (*Official Report*, Vol. 364, col. 1530).
41. Mr Duff Cooper, speaking in London last night, dealt with the use of internees for anti-Nazi propaganda against Germany, and said: 'I hope a great many of those who have been interned are being released for that purpose.' (*Manchester Guardian*, 23 August 1940)
42. House of Commons, 22 August 1940 (*Official Report*, Vol. 364, col. 1554).
43. House of Lords, 5 September 1940 (*Official Report*, Vol. 117, col. 373).
44. Cmd. 6233, *Civilian Internees of Enemy Nationality (Revised)*, October 1940.
45. House of Commons, 26 November 1940 (*Official Report*, Vol. 367, col. 80).
46. When the question of physical assault on refugees by fascists was raised in the House of Commons on 28 November, Mr Morrison expressed his hope that 'the majority of anti-Nazis will hold their ground, will do something. Physical assault is one matter, but in the matter of contagion of opinion, I hope the anti-Nazis will do their share of propaganda' (*Official Report*, Vol. 367, cols 305–6).
47. House of Commons, 3 December 1940 (*Official Report*, Vol. 367, col. 499).
48. See Note 6, p. 96, above.
49. House of Commons, 19 December 1940 (*Official Report*, Vol. 367, col. 1325).

50. The number of releases, explained Mr Morrison in the House of Commons on 3 December 1940, 'includes all, whether non-Fascists or Fascists, or whatever their categories are' (*Official Report*, Vol. 367, col. 451).
51. Cmd. 6120, *Papers Concerning the Treatment of German Nationals in Germany, 1938–1939.*

What Use Are the Refugees?

A military defeat of the German people cannot in itself ensure the overthrow of fascism in Europe and would mean either direct foreign domination or national rulers chosen by and subservient to the interests of the victorious foreign powers. Unless the German people themselves bring about the overthrow of Hitler and determine their own future rule, such an outcome to the struggle will not satisfy them any better than foreign domination satisfies the peoples of such countries as Czechoslovakia and France today. Europe would breed a generation pledged to future wars of revenge and liberation.

Every move that links the people of Germany to Nazi rule by demonstrating a desire for their destruction *as a people* and does not uphold the principle of peoples deciding freely upon their own rule, released from the fear of internal oppression or foreign domination, is a move to consolidate fascism, even though German cities are razed to the ground and European populations starved to death.

A generation of young Germans bred in the Nazi faith will not be won away from that allegiance by the military force of a foreign power. That force may physically destroy or temporarily subdue them, but in the fullness of time there will be thrown up new Hitlers to 'liberate' Germany once more. Not the voice of foreign guns, but that of their own compatriots determined to win their rights and liberties on their own soil will weaken Hitler's hold on them. The Nazis were forced to resort to foreign aggression to stave off growing discontent at home. Having ascended to power on the 'wrongs of Versailles', Hitler has drafted the wrongs of Compiègne which, while producing untold misery for the French people, has in no way improved the lot of the Germans. But what reason has anyone for supposing that they would prefer a new Versailles?

Plainly, the alternative to Compiègne and Hitler's New Order is not Versailles and Britain's Old Order, but the defeat of fascism by the peoples living under fascism.

It is not within the power of exiles to overthrow fascist rule in their own countries and replace it by a system of democratic government. That is a task of such magnitude that it can only be brought about by the concerted efforts of the majority of the people and as a result of their ceaseless struggle according to the situation prevailing in their own countries. The one thing exiles must not do is to embark upon a policy of their own, unrelated to the prevailing situation of their own people; still less must they abandon their political independence by serving foreign interests.

The political refugees from Germany are the comrades and fellow-fighters of those who work in Germany for the overthrow of Hitler. Their mission is that of their fellows inside Germany. It is not their mission to work for the foreign domination of Germany. They cannot be party to the aims of foreign powers unless these are explicitly identical with their own. Their aims are simply and solely the overthrow of Hitlerism in Germany by the German people. Their role in exile is to further those aims by every means legitimately open to them; to keep their integrity, their courage, their vision and their convictions unimpaired that they may be fit to join their people and participate in the building of a free Germany of the future; they must learn to know and serve the peoples among whom they find themselves in every way that does not entail the sacrifice of their purpose and probity. So with the Austrians, the Sudeten and the Czech refugees. To suggest that they should place themselves unreservedly at the disposition of governments whose spokesmen openly advocate the destruction of the German people (since they failed to come to terms with the oppressors of that people), is to suggest that the refugees are men without purpose or honour in their own country.

How terribly the cause of the exiles may be betrayed was shown in France, where the Czech Army fought and died for Laval and Co. President Beneš' official paper *Čechoslovák v Anglii* stated on 28 June 1940:

> The men at the wheel, who led us to Munich by betraying the Franco-Czech alliance have continued their Staviskyade throughout the war

> and did not even spare the British Empire in their betrayal. History knows no example of such abominable conduct, there is no precedent for that malignant Fifth Column who, terrified of a political upheaval, terrified of losing power, disheartened by the bitterness of the struggle against Hitler, have surrendered both themselves and their foreign helpers, their own allies, to the revenge of the Nazi German bloodsuckers.

The deep disillusionment expressed in this passage was the inevitable reward of those Czech leaders who had placed themselves, and called their compatriots to arms, under the government which had betrayed the Franco-Czech alliance at Munich, despite the refusal of that government to give so much as a guarantee that this Czech Legion on its soil would not be fighting for war aims which included the restoration of the Hapsburg monarchy.

Nevertheless, this realisation has not prevented foreign governments from being formed in Britain and placing themselves under the protection and at the service of a government whose war and peace aims have not been defined. Sir Edward Grigg said:

> We are responsible for our relations with certain sovereign Governments at present domiciled in this country. It is in accordance with our principles to show them the greatest consideration and respect, and all the more so ... because they are at this time in distress and to some extent dependent upon our good offices for their very life.[1]

How far these governments, which have no mandate from their peoples and are dependent on a foreign power for 'their very life' will, after the war, represent the aspirations of those peoples rather than those of that foreign power is a matter which must exercise the mind of every responsible refugee in Britain.

> The foreign governments ... are not *de facto* Governments on any territory of their own. They are societies or assemblies of friendly foreigners temporarily domiciled in this country. They are in no way the properly constituted Government of the country which they represent. They are no longer amenable to the Constitution which appointed them ... and certainly not all of them are even a quorum of the Government which existed at the time their countries were overrun ...

said Sir Joseph Nall in the Debate on the Allied Forces Bill.[2]

Provisional governments which are formed undemocratically on foreign soil and accept a state of dependence on a foreign power thereby demonstrate that they have ceased to rely on the strength of their own people at home. For those refugees, however, whose faith in the ultimate victory of democratic forces *inside* their country has not been shattered, the paramount need is to retain their political independence, subject only to the demands of the living anti-fascist opposition at home, and to steer clear of the sunken rocks of foreign allegiance upon which political integrity must sooner or later founder.

Ah, just as we thought, the reader will say: the refugees are not to help the British people in their hour of need. Even if we free them from internment, they are to remain aloof with their political purity while we do the working and the fighting.

Not so. There is no danger and no hardship that the British civil population suffers in this war which the refugees would not and do not share. Every form of Civil Defence and of industrial and agricultural production should be open to them; their scientists, their doctors and their nurses should be mobilised to save the lives of English air-raid victims, as we saved the lives of the refugees. Their architects and builders should work for our homeless, as we made homes for them; they should grow food for those who fed them; they should live as our people do, and among them, and form those ties of shared experience in days of stress upon which a better understanding between the peoples of a free Europe can be founded.

It would be possible to show how even under the most unfavourable circumstances the refugees have made tremendous efforts to equip themselves with knowledge and experience, and have demonstrated their unquenchable desire to retain their physical and mental fitness. Indeed, this has been done in many journals.

The refugees' behaviour in internment, where their social life and reactions were isolated and observable as under a bell-jar, proved this fact. Although of different classes, education and interests, all the anti-Nazis in the camps elected and accepted a democratic leadership from amongst themselves ('camp fathers' and camp committees – not 'camp fuehrers') and set up remarkable camp universities in which full use was made of the distinguished scholars and teachers amongst the internees; technical as well as academic subjects were given an important place in the planned curricula, while the general cultural life in the camps reached an extremely high standard. In all cases, while it is to be noted that these activities could not have existed (as they did not exist in concentration camps in Germany) without the approval or at least the tolerance of the camp officials, the initiative came in all cases from the refugees who sometimes mapped out ambitious courses of study before it was known whether they would be allowed the use of paper, pencils or books. While the lack of news – at all times regarded as the most intolerable feature of their position – obviously had a depressing effect on the spirits of the internees, demoralisation never spread through a whole camp and was least in evidence where the refugees had themselves organised their camp life.

This attitude manifested itself, whenever it was given a chance and a lead, throughout the refugee era; a book could be written on that era in the terms of the refugees' own efforts and achievements.

This book is not concerned with that aspect of refugee life, but with the external policies and conditions which shaped their experiences.

The terrible stories of refugee life in internment camps and deportation ships have been recorded in speeches and newspapers of the time. For those who heard and read, the desire to alleviate so much distress sprang up spontaneously and joined that other steady and generous stream of humanitarianism which has flowed since 1933 from the refugee aid organisations.

But there comes a point when palliative measures, however important, seem dwarfed by the magnitude of the sufferings they seek to relieve. It is as though we gave the patient every anodyne but failed to diagnose his disease. Only by understanding the causes of the suffering will the British people be able to give the refugees, in the last resort, the help they need. For years we have neglected that question, allowing the right of asylum to be trampled on, the right to work to be denied, the right to a recognised status for our friends amongst the victims and opponents of Hitler to be ignored, failing to see that these are rights which a democratic people ignores, denies and tramples on at its peril.

France has taught us that.

The friends and sympathisers of the refugees who have lived closest to their problem have become inured to the fundamental illiberalism of official policy. They have worked within its provisions, which they were forced to accept as an indispensable condition of their work – itself a triumph of tenacity and goodwill. The pity is that, in the turmoil of the day-to-day problems, their attention was diverted from the basic issues. They bore, in inexhaustible patience, with the difficulties created by the government regulations; they sang the praises of every government official who provided a narrow loophole for the work of rescue and rehabilitation. Throughout the years they raised and kept aloft a brave banner of decency and humanity in the shameful wastes of acquiescence to Nazi bestiality. But that is not enough. The matter was always too big for little companies of humanitarians, because it was never an isolated question, but one that was closely bound up with British policy as a whole.

The relationship of the refugee question with British policy at home and abroad as a whole always lurked behind the smaller issues presented by the refugees. As the attack upon them sharpened and came into the open, this relationship revealed itself unmistakably.

Side by side with the British people, the refugees have lived and suffered, always a little worse off, always bearing the brunt of the moves to lower standards and to curtail liberties. In championing the cause of the refugees, we take a stand for our own democratic rights; in fighting for these we vindicate the refugees.

NOTES

1. House of Commons, 21 August 1940 (*Official Report*, Vol. 364, col. 1410).
2. House of Commons, 21 August 1940 (*Official Report*, Vol. 364, cols 1407–8).

Index